AF725116

FIVE TRILLION DOLLARS

and

EVER-DEEPER IN DEBT

FIVE TRILLION DOLLARS

and

EVER-DEEPER IN DEBT

A NEW NET WORTH TAX IN 1995

IS OUR NATION'S ONLY WAY OUT

(WITH DEBT AMORTIZATION AND TAX TABLES)

by

James G. Miles

September, 1994

Manufactured in the United States of America
ISBN 0-8062-5151-4

Library of Congress Cataloging-in-Process Data
Miles, James G.
Five Trillion Dollars and Ever-Deeper In Debt
National Debt
Federal Debt
Federal Deficit
Economic Policy

Wholesale and retail dealer inquiries invited.
Call Carlton Press Corp. 1-800-BOOKS-08
for more information.

**This book is addressed to all voters
and all candidates
for the U.S. Senate
and House of Representatives
in 1994.**

**It is dedicated to
all children and grandchildren
in the United States.**

FIVE TRILLION DOLLARS

and

EVER-DEEPER IN DEBT

FOREWORD

What have we here, in the United States of America, at the beginning of September, 1994?

It is less than ten weeks to the Congressional elections this fall, and Congress is more uncertain and quarrelsome than ever trying to decide on a Federal budget for 1995. There isn't enough money, or "pork", to go around. Most-needed programs get delayed, cut or cancelled.

Meanwhile, the Federal Reserve Bank (the central bank of the U.S.) raised interest rates it controls for the fifth time this year, for a total of 1 3/4%). Major banks have followed suit by raising their prime rates they charge their most favored and reliable customers by 1 3/4% up to 7 3/4%. Home mortgage, automobile load and credit rates are up even more, by 2 1/2%, as retail lenders take their additional bites.

All this causes higher prices and true inflation affecting all customers and older people on fixed incomes.

The stock market has fallen nearly 6% since the first of the year, and is exceedingly sensitive to interest rates.

Millions of previously laid-off people are finding jobs. But at much lower wages than they previously had.

The U.S. dollar is in deep trouble. It has fallen to the lowest exchange rate against major currencies since World War II. The central banks of sixteen countries have stepped in to prop up the dollar, but they are not succeeding.

The economy as measured by Gross Domestic Product (GDP) grew at the annualized rate of 3.4% in the past eight months. But the Federal Debt grew even faster (at the rate of 6% annually).

At September 1, 1994, the Debt reached an all-time high of $4.645 trillion. The unpaid debt and the interest on it are increasing every day.

It is important to note that this awesome situation is not the fault of President Bill Clinton, although it falls on the shoulders of his Administration to correct it.

The rapid increase in the National Debt started in 1970 (during the Vietnam War) when Nixon lowered top marginal income taxes by 37%. Reagan lowered them by another 17% in 1988.

Meanwhile, the Federal Debt grew twelve-fold. From $354 billion to $4.4 trillion at the end of Bush's Administration.

Clinton won a meager 6.6% top marginal income tax tax increase in 1993, but that was far short of being enough to fix the problem.

So the Debt continues to increase, *ad infinitum*. Until a different solution is found.

Your author has three objectives in writing this book:

1) Provide complete and up-to-date information to the American people as to the true nature and danger of the Federal Debt and the problems it is creating.

2) Propose a solution to get this country out of debt in six to ten years.

3) Propose an across-the-board, multipartison voter-driven election in November, 1994, to elect candidates to Congress who will support debt treduction.

I am not your usual degreed, board-certified, theoretical economist. Neither am I a politician. Therefore, I am free to develop unusual solutions to problems.

I am "retired" after over fifty years in business... from the outset of the computer industry, in which I was one of the pioneers and a worldwide salesman.

I have no ax to grind except to help this country understand and solve its greatest problem...our overwhelming, ever-increasing Federal debt.

In this book, I have assembled and presented as briefly as possible, at least *quantitative summaries* of the essential facts regarding the debt problem, its consequences, and its solution. Because of my concentration on the debt subject, I have omitted dozens of *qualitative societal issues* I would have liked to have included, and left those issues to sociologists, health, and education experts.

Between politicians and the media, the debt subject has been almost totally avoided to date. It is almost as if there is a "conspiracy of silence" on the subject.

However, the data is available as reported herein from named sources. And a large-scale equitable solution is at hand.

Fortunately, I have never been in deep debt. But I certainly can recognize dangerous debt when I see it. And the United States *is* dangerously in debt at the present time.

This book is written in three parts:

I. **The problem** that we as a country now have, and must face by the end of 1996 when our Federal debt will exceed $5 trillion (from whence we are headed toward national bankruptcy).

II. **The solution** to the problem...A Net Worth Tax is the only way to put a stop to continual giant deficits that are literally sucking away our way of life. And that of other children, our children and grandchildren.

III. **The needed bipartisan political action** to be initiated by all of us in the Congressional elections in 1994.

CONSTITUTION OF THE UNITED STATES

(Preamble)

"We the People of the United States,
in Order to form a more perfect Union,
establish Justice,
insure domestic Tranquillity,
provide for the common defense,
promote the general Welfare, and
secure the Blessings of Liberty
to ourselves and our Posterity,
do ordain and establish this Constitution
for the United States of America."

Signed: George Washington, James Madison, Benjamin Franklin, Alexander Hamilton and 35 others. (1787)

Author's comments:

In my mind's eye, I can see those Fathers of our country sitting around a table, checking-off the subjects they considered most important. And arranging them in the order of importance.

It is particularly interesting to see which words they capitalized, and which words they did not.

Take time to go over those words again.
Note the action verbs they used.
Think about them.

According to their hopes, how well are we doing?

Winston Churchill wrote:

" There are two ways in which a gigantic debt may be spread over new decades and future generations. There is a right and healthy way. And there is a wrong and morbid way.

" The wrong way is to fail to make the utmost provision for amortisation which prudence allows, to aggravate the burden of the debt by fresh borrowings, and to live from hand to mouth and from year to year.

" And to exclaim with Louis XVI, 'After me, the deluge!'"

$5 TRILLION DOLLARS AND EVER-DEEPER IN DEBT

Why this particular title for this book?

Because the Federal debt at September 1, 1994, is already $4.645 trillion. And President Clinton's Fiscal Year 1995 Budget projects it will reach $5 trillion by the end of 1996.

That is only 2 1/2 years away from the writing of this book.

That's barely enough time to...

Elect a new Congress in this election year, 1994 to...

Establish a new set of tax laws in 1995, based on equitable Net Worth Taxes, proposed herein in order to...

Avoid national bankruptcy, due to ever-increasing debt.

How did the debt get that large?

How dangerous is it to our country?

How do we bail ourselves out?

Why the urgency?

The following pages tell the story.

FACING REALITY

THE DEBT is something no one in official Washington wants to talk about.

Not Presidents, not Cabinet Members;

Not the Senate, not the House of Representatives;

Not Democrats;

Most certainly not Republicans who are unanimously holding to their "no more taxes" position, which is the main part of the problem.

Unless the United States changes direction, we are on the road to certain national bankruptcy.

Budgeting and rebudgeting until we're blue in the face simply will not reduce or eliminate the debt.

We must find another way.

THE BALLOT-BOX SOLUTION

In the 1994 Congressional elections, WE...that means all of us together, cooperatively... Democrats, Republicans, Independents and followers of Ross Perot...must elect a Congress who will commit, in advance, to establish a new set of tax laws in 1994 and 1995. These laws would start the process of amortizing (paying off) the free falling Federal debt...

> (Exactly as you would your mortgage, unless you want to lose your home).

Unless and until that is done, there is no way we can get rid of the deficit, balance the budget and get back on a reasonable track.

PRINCIPAL SOURCES OF DATA FOR THIS BOOK

* *Budgets of the United States Government for Fiscal Years 1994 and 1995, with Appendices and historical tables,* President's Office of Management and Budget.

* *Economic Report of the President,* 2/14/94.

* *Treasury Bulletins,* Office of the Secretary, Treasury Department (Quarterly, Weekly, Daily 1993, 1994).

* Department of the Treasury, Public Information Office, for today's amount of the Federal Debt. (Tel. 202-219-3303).

* Federal Reserve Board of Governors' Publications:
    - *Balance Sheets for the U.S. Economy 1945-1993,* Table C.9, *Flow of Funds,* March 9, 1994
    - *Monetary Policy Reports* to Congress and its Committees, 1994
    - *Reports of Shadow Open Market Committee to FRB,* 1994

* Internal Revenue Service *Statistics of Income Bulletins and Reports,* Spring, 1994.

* *1993 Statistical Abstract of the United States,* U.S. Department of Commerce.

* *1993 Green Book - Overview of Entitlement Programs,* Committee on Ways and Means, U.S. House of Representatives, 7/7/93.

* *Facts and Figures on Government Finance, 1993 Edition,* by Tax Foundation (a private sector not-for-profit foundation) Washington, D.C.

* *New York Times, Barrons Market Week, Wall Street Journal,* and other leading news publications.

* *Encyclopedia Britannica, 1993.*

DATA PRESENTATION

As used throughout this book...

Most dollar amounts are *then-current dollars* according to the year when transactions were made and reported by U.S. Government Departments.

The Federal gross debt includes consolidated short-term and long-term debts outstanding (including Treasury "borrowings" via bonds, bills and notes and from the Social Security Trust Fund and other designated funds).

The numbers we're dealing with are so huge that (for reasons of clarity and ease of understanding) most data herein are rounded to the nearest 2 or 3 decimal places. This does not destroy basic validity, and conforms to accepted accounting practices. (For all practical purposes, the rounded plusses and minuses offset each other).

THE BASIC UNCOMPROMISING ARITHMETIC

Many people have a hard time understanding the enormous size of the numbers involved. This may help...

10	x 1 hundred	=	1 thousand, or 10^3
1,000	x 1 thousand	=	1 million, or 10^6
1,000	x 1 million	=	1 billion, or 10^9
1,000	x 1 billion	=	1 trillion, or 10^{12}

This arithmetic applies to anything
...from dollars of household net worth
...to dollars of debt.

Keep this table in mind. We'll come back to it.

"DEFICIT OR DEBT"?
WHAT ARE WE TALKING ABOUT?

The annual deficit is the amount of money the U.S. Government loses each year. It is the short-fall between income (from taxes), and spending (for expenses and programs).

The Federal Debt, usually called "The National Debt" is the sum total of all Federal deficits or losses since the signing of the U.S. Constitution in 1787.

The present Federal Budget projects a $176 billion deficit (or loss) in 1994, increasing to a projected $201 billion loss in 1999.

Meanwhile, the Federal Debt will have grown by those same amounts, yearly.

Those numbers are what this book is all about.

THE CONSTITUTIONAL BASIS FOR THE BUDGET

Article I, Section 7 of the United States Constitution reads:
"All Bills for raising Revenue shall originate in the House of Representatives; but the Senate may propose or concur with Amendments as on other bills...and...be presented to the President of the United States; if he approves he shall sign it, but if not he shall return it, with his objections to that House in which it shall have originated..."

Thus it is established that all branches of Government, (the President, the House of Representatives and the Senate) are jointly responsible for the budgeting process.

Therefore, blame for budgetary policy cannot be placed solely on either branch of the government or on either major political party.

BUDGETING PROCEDURE

To simplify the budgeting process, in 1974, Congress established the *Office of Management and Budget (OMB)* as part of the Office of the President.

Each year, the Office of Management and Budget...

1) Updates dollar-amounts from the previous fiscal year (FY);
2) Prepares the budget for the upcoming fiscal year;
3) Projects the budget for four additional years.

Calendarwise, the U.S. Fiscal Year extends from October 1st of any given calendar year, to September 30th of the next.

The President forwards the *Budget*-proposal to Congress for its review and approval...or disapproval.

Congress has its own *Congressional Budget Office (CBO)*, which reviews the budget items as submitted by the President, taking into account Congress' political objectives. Accordingly, the CBO often arrives at different results from those submitted by the OMB.

Usually, the Joint House and Senate Committee on the Budget spends three or four months debating the budget proposal.

When it has reached substantial agreement, the Committee publishes its *Conference Report* for distribution to all members of the House and Senate for full floor debate.

FIVE TRILLION DOLLARS

and

EVER-DEEPER IN DEBT

PART I
THE PROBLEM

FIVE TRILLION DOLLARS

and

EVER-DEEPER IN DEBT

THE PRIMARY CAUSE OF THE INCREASES IN THE FEDERAL DEFICIT AND FEDERAL DEBT

Roosevelt had run U.S. participation throughout all of World War II by controlling inflation (using a tight set of price controls) and maintaining top marginal income taxes at 94% on all incomes over $200,000 throughout WW II. These policies resulted in only a $200 billion increase in debt, so that WW II ended with only $260 billion national debt.

After WW II, Truman, with his "buck stops here" attitude, continued to run the U.S. with a very tight fiscal policy. He kept personal income taxes substantially at WW II rates throughout his term in office, during which he allowed them to drop only 6%, from 94% to 88% (top marginal).

Presidents Eisenhower, Kennedy, and Johnson kept top marginal income tax rates at the 87% level, and ran substantially balanced budgets (see Table, p.18). However, Johnson ran a $22 billion deficit in 1968 due to the high cost of the Vietnam War.

In contrast with his five high-taxing predecessors, and with the expensive and intractable Vietnam War continuing with no end in sight, President Nixon, in 1969, in an almost unbelievable move, initiated the reduction of maximum marginal personal income taxes from 87% to 70% to 50% by 1971. This, notwithstanding the continuing high costs of that war through 1973.

The direct result: from 1970 through 1974 alone, the Federal debt increased from $354 billion to $486 billion.

That tax-reduction initiative by Nixon immediately triggered the debt-landslide that continued through the next 25 years of Ford, Carter, Reagan and Bush. Those debt results are still spinning out of control. (Sources, see tables pp. 18 and 19, and graph, p. 20).

GROWTH OF THE FEDERAL DEBT WITH INCREASES IN ANNUAL DEFICITS DUE TO REDUCTIONS OF INCOME TAXES 1970-1992

Sources:

- Treasury Department, Table A18. *Gross Debt, Federal Government, 1945-1993.*
- Office of Management and Budget and Treasury Department, Table C1. *Summary of Federal Fiscal Operations, 1945-1993.*
- Treasury Department, Table C36. *Federal Individual Income Tax Rates, 1944-1993.*
- Clinton's FY'94 and FY'95 Budgets, and Historical Tables thereto.
- U.S. Treasury Public Information Office

Fiscal Years	Administration Party	Income Tax Top Marginal Rates Per Household Percent	National Deficits (losses) $ Billions	National Debt $ Billions
1945	Truman	94 %	48	260
to	Democrat			
	WW II to 9/45			
1952	Korean War 1950-1953	88 %	2	260
1953	Eisenhower	88 %	6	266
'54	Republican	87 %	5	271
'55		87 %	3	274
'56		87%	0	274
'57		87%	1	275
'58		87 %	1	276
'59		87%	8	284
'60		87 %	2	286
1961	Kennedy	87 %	3	289
'62	Democrat	87 %	9	298
1963	Johnson	87 %	8	306
'64	Vietnam War starts	87 %	6	312
'65		87 %	5	317
'66		87 %	3	320
'67		87 %	6	326
'68		87 %	22	348

GROWTH OF THE NATIONAL DEBT WITH INCREASES IN ANNUAL DEFICITS DUE TO REDUCTIONS OF INCOME TAXES 1969-1988

Sources: Same as page 5.

Fiscal Years	Administration Party	Income Tax Top Marginal Rates Per Household Percent	National Deficit $ Billions	National Debt $ Billions
1969	Nixon	87 %	6	354
'70	Republican	70 %	17	371
'71	(Vietnam War	50 %	27	398
'72	continues,	50 %	29	427
'73	ends)	50 %	41	468
'74	Nixon resigns	50 %	18	486
'75	Ford	50 %	58	544
'76		50 %	87	631
1977	Carter	50 %	78	709
'78	Democrat	50 %	71	780
'79		50 %	70	850
'80		50 %	64	914
1981	Reagan	50 %	90	1,004
'82	Republican	50 %	143	1,147
'83		50 %	235	1,382
'84		50 %	195	1,577
'85		50%	250	1,827
'86		50 %	303	2,130
'87		50 %	224	2,354
'88		33 %	261	2,615
1989	Bush	33 %	266	2,881
'90	Republican	33 %	385	3,266
'91		33 %	417	3,683
'92		33 %	382	4,065
FY'93 to end, Bush Actual		33 %	346	4,411
1994	Clinton Budget	39.6 %	235	4,646
'95	Democrat	39.6 %	176	4,822
'96	projections	---	173	4,995
'97	"	---	181	5,176
'98	"	---	187	5,363
'99	"	---	201	5,564

GROWTH OF THE NATIONAL DEBT AND THE PRIMARY REASON FOR IT

This a graphical plot of the data tabulated on pp. 18-19. It shows how the National Debt increased after the Nixon tax cuts in 1970 during the Vietnam War, and thereafter.

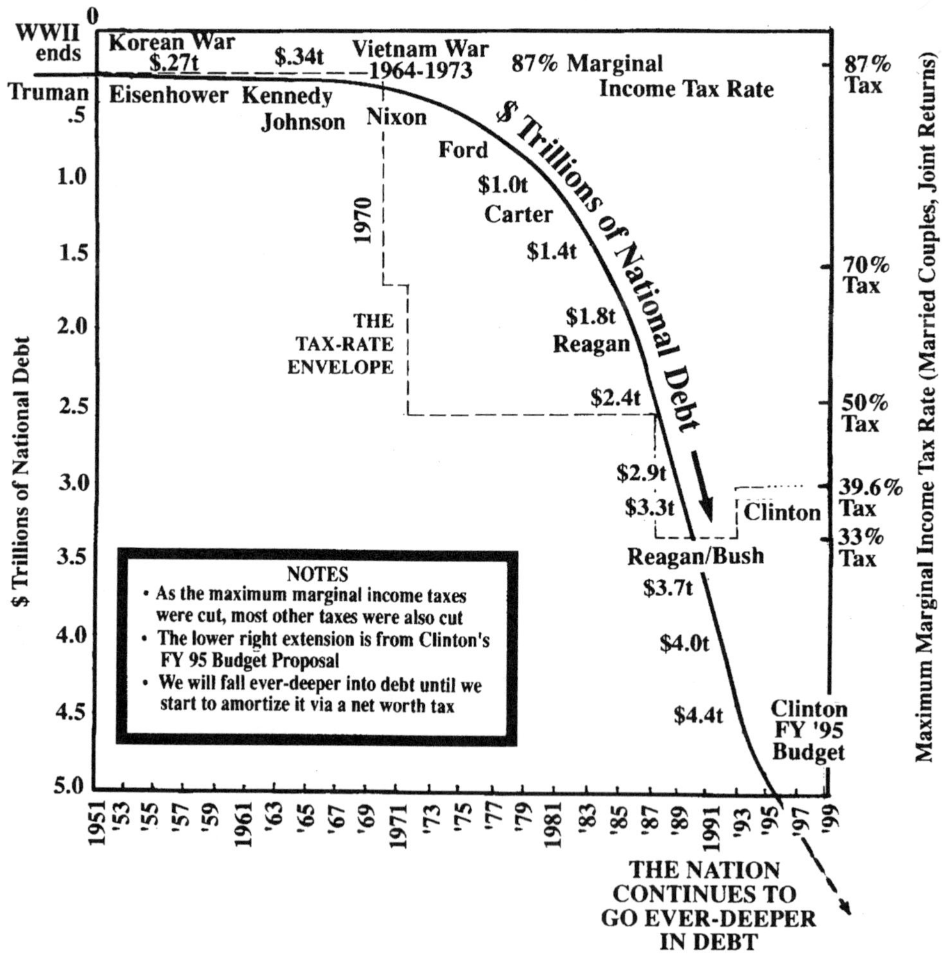

GROWTH OF THE FEDERAL DEBT AND THE PRIMARY REASON FOR IT... NIXONOMICS AND REAGANOMICS

The motivation for Nixon's tax-reduction-initiatives was his belief in the Keynesian economic theories advanced by Lord John Maynard Keynes of England in the 1930s. *"We are all Keynesians now."* declared Nixon in 1971 (Investor's Business Daily 4/23/94).

The principles of those theories were: Reduce taxes on the wealthy, who will then, supposedly, have more after-tax cash to expand their businesses. More jobs will thereby, hopefully, be created... Thus (hopefully) the economy will improve.

Accordingly, from 1969-1971, Reagan reduced top marginal income taxes by 37%...(from 87% down to 50%.)

Well-intentioned as Nixon, Reagan, and Bush may have been in following Keynesian economic theories... when their economic goals weren't being achieved after 16 years of reduced taxes, Reagan, and the Congress, reduced marginal top income taxes again. This time from 50% down to 33%.

Because of diminished tax income to the Treasury, the deficit increased.

Even-deeper Federal debt was the inevitable result.

See Graph on page 20.

(Sources: Same as top of table, p. 18.)

PRESIDENT BUSH'S FY'93 BUDGET

1/28/92: President Bush gave his last Annual *State of the Union* Address to the joint House and Senate. **He didn't mention the Federal debt.** (Source: Congressional Record, 1/28/93)

The following day, Bush presented Congress his $1,468 billion budget, projecting a $317 billion deficit. He continued to follow the Nixonomics/Reaganomics doctrine to the letter.

10/6/92: After more than 8 months of give and take with Congress, President Bush finally signed off on the final portion of the FY'93 budget, (to become Public Law 102-377-396).

By the end of September, 1993 (when all the numbers were in) Bush was $29 billion over his own budget, bringing the FY'93 deficit to $346 billion, and the Federal Debt to $4.411 trillion.

(Sources:
1) Bush's Office of Management and Budget, 1/29/92;
2) Congressional Quarterly, 10/7/92;
3) Treasury Department, Public Information Office, Washington, D.C., tel. 202-219-3303, 10/10/93)

SOCIAL SECURITY TRUST FUND BORROWINGS AND OTHER TRUST FUNDS

From 1981, the Reagan/Bush Administrations started a new cash-raising process for general governmental spending by "borrowing" heavily from the several *trust funds* that had been set up to protect people. They borrowed most heavily from the *Old-Age, Survivors, Disability and Health Insurance Trust Fund* (commonly known as the *Social Security Trust Fund)* which ended a total of $454 billion in the hole at the end of FY'93.

A total of $406 billion of additional borrowings from other trust funds took place during the Reagan/Bush years. These were principally from *Federal Employees Retirement Funds* and *National Service Life Insurance Funds.*

Both houses of Congress and Presidents signed off on all these "borrowings" year-by-year, as they accumulated.

The Treasury Department includes these $860 billion "borrowings" among the items of gross Federal debt.

Note: The trust fund borrowing practice is continuing (using a different nomenclature) in the Clinton FY'95 Budget. It is under the title of so-called "Invested Balances," which, translated, means *invested in U.S. Debt Securities* (bonds, notes and bills).

For the Social Security and Medical Trust Funds alone, these borrowings are projected to increase by an average of $86 billion per year through FY'99. That will leave the Treasury owing those funds over $1 trillion by the end of this century.

(Sources:
Treasury Department *Composition of the Federal Debt by Type of Obligation,* via Tax Foundation Table C62, p.148.
FY'95 Budget of the U.S. Government, Historical Tables, pp.229-230.)

Author's comment:
True, those Trust Funds need to be invested *somewhere* (and I'd prefer U.S. Securities to the stock market!). But the problem is... with an aging population... where will the money come from to pay their Social Security benefits???

GROWTH OF FOREIGN DEBT

Starting 1989, the Bush Administration increasingly borrowed from foreign sources via sales of U.S. Bonds and Notes.

The total amount of foreign debt outstanding at the end of FY'93 was $1.15 trillion. This makes the United States the largest debtor-nation in the world.

(Source: *Treasury Bulletin, Summary of Federal Debt, June, 1994, Table FD-1, page 31, and IFS, p. 77.)*

EFFECT OF U.S. DEBT INTERNATIONALLY

The International Banking Community has been alarmed for many years about the United States' increasing budget deficits and increasing Federal debt. The Community perceives that we are not doing enough to solve our financial problems.

As long ago as 1981-1983, Paul Volker, Chairman of the Federal Reserve Board during the Reagan years, wrote stiff warnings on this subject.

The International Monetary Fund (IMF), headquartered in Washington, D.C., is a specialized agency of the United Nations. It's members are pledged to maintain orderly currency arrangements. The U.S. is a member.

Member countries with temporary financial difficulties may, upon application, borrow funds from the IMF and may negotiate lines of credit in anticipation of actual needs. Criteria for borrowing from the IMF include how well a country is (or is not) bringing its budget deficits and debt under control.

If the United States should become bankrupt, and should therefore need to go to the International Monetary Fund for loans, this country's inability to manage and amortize its debts would be a discouraging factor to the IMF and would probably disqualify the United States as a borrower.

(Source: Federal Reserve Board , International Finance Division, 4/7/94, direct to author.)

CLINTON'S BUDGETS FOR FISCAL YEARS 1994 AND 1995

January 20, 1993: William J. Clinton was sworn into office as the 42d President of the United States. Albert A. Gore was sworn in as his Vice President.

Clinton and Gore were pre-ordained to carry the burden of hundreds of unattended-to societal and infrastructure needs.

In addition, they had to shoulder the then-awesome $4.411 trillion national debt accumulated or committed by Reagan and Bush.

April 8, 1993: President Clinton sent his $1,515 billion budget proposal for FY'94 to the House and Senate. *Incrementally,* it was only $18 billion more than Bush's FY'93 actualized $1,497 billion budget, with its deficit.

(Sources: Treasury Dept. Public Information Office in re Bush's FY'93 deficit; Clinton's 4/8/93 FY'94 Budget Proposal.)

> Senate Republicans immediately rejected Clinton's Budget Proposal, on the grounds that it made a small move toward budget-balancing by increasing estate taxes slightly, and by increasing top incremental income taxes by 6.6% (from Reagan/Bush's 33% up to 39.6%). And was retroactive to January 1, 1993.

According to Law, Clinton's Budget Proposal was routed to the House/Senate Conference Committee on the Budget (H.R. 2264).

For three long months, the Joint Conference Committee (both parties) negotiated and traded "pork" by-the-barrel-full for their constituents.

(Source: Omnibus Budget Reconciliation Act of 1993, Conference Report on the Budget, House of Representatives to Accompany H.R. 2264.)

August 4, 1993: The Joint Conference Committee passed its H.R. 2264 *Compromise Conference Report,* and ordered it to be printed and sent to the full House and Senate.

August 5, 1993: For 12 hours, the full House of Representatives heatedly debated the Conference Report on the Budget.

> Before TV cameras, they acted their parts well for the benefit of their campaign-funders...Also, to show their voting-constituencies how strongly they oppose **any** attempt to increase taxes on their hard-won earnings. I watched it all on television.

Late that evening the full House finally voted 218-216 to pass the Bill. **Not a single Republican voted in favor.**

Titled H.R. 103-213, the Bill was sent to the Senate.

August 6, 1993: The full Senate similarly argued about the budget for 12 hours...

> As *anchor-speaker* for Republicans, Senate Minority Leader, Robert Dole of Kansas had himself "done-up" by a beauty operator for the forthcoming greatest photo-op of his political career (New York Times photo and text 8/7/93).

Quoting directly from the *Congressional Record-Senate August 6, 1993, pp. S10711-S10713*...Senator Dole "drew a line in the sand" and began his closing argument for the Republican Senate Delegation as follows:

> "All Americans watching television on CNN and C-Span, put down your remote controls and grab your wallets because your taxes are about to go up"...
>
> "I thank the American people for their efforts in trying to defeat this terrible tax bill"...
>
> "I wish my colleagues well when they try to explain why they voted for this package"...
>
> "What this bill has done is underscore the difference between the Republican Party and the Democratic Party and the philosophies of Democrats and Republicans"...
>
> "You are going to have retroactive tax rate increases"...
>
> "Your estate tax is going to affect the families, the heirs"...
>
> "President Clinton may well go down in history as the only President who increased taxes before he took office"...

> "I believe this is a bad plan. It raises taxes and it does little to ...control the deficit. That is why I am voting against it. That is why all 43 of my Republican colleagues are voting against it"...
>
> **"We Republicans do not raise taxes"...**

Senate Republican Minority Leader Dole did not mention one word about the Federal debt in his epic nationally-televised speech.

The Republican leader's time having expired, Vice President Gore (in his capacity as President of the Senate), assigned the podium to Senator George J. Mitchell, from Maine, the Democrat Senate Majority Leader, for the remaining four minutes of the debate on the *Conference Report*. Mitchell countered Senator Dole's arguments...

Vice President Gore: "All time has expired. The question is on the adoption of the conference report on H.R. 2264, *The Budget Reconciliation Act*"..."The yeas and nays are ordered. The clerk will call the roll".

The legislative clerk called the roll.

The result: 50 "nay" votes were cast versus 50 "yea" votes.

All Republicans voted "nay", as did six Democrats.

Vice President Al Gore cast the tie-breaking vote, causing the Bill to pass by a margin of one vote.

The Bill was sent to the President for signing.

(Source: *Congressional Record--Senate,* August 6, 1993).

The next day, August 7, 1993, the *Congressional Quarterly*, reported:

> *"This was the only time in post-war congressional history that all members of either party had voted unanimously against any Bill of any kind."*

August 10, 1993: President Clinton signed the FY '94 Budget in to Law (identified as P.L. 103-66.) It included a top marginal income tax rate increase of 6.6%, (from 33% to 39.6%).

January 25, 1994: Immediately following President Clinton's State of the Union Message, in a pre-taped nationally televised rebuttal, Senator Bob Dole spoke again for the Republicans. He proclaimed that Clinton's FY '94 budget was "the largest tax increase in American history", and he boasted that the increase had been opposed by "every Republican in the House and Senate."
(Sources: My tape recording and *USA Today*, 1/26/94.)

Dole also alleged that "There is no health care crisis in America."

Dole either did not have the facts or he was being intellectually-dishonest because he failed to mention that top income taxes had been hiked from 15% up to 67% at the start of WWI in 1917. And from 79% up to 94% at the start of WWII.

The meager 6.6% tax *increase* for FY '94 was but a small increment to recover part of the 54% income tax decrement from 87% down to 33% from 1969-1993 under Nixon/Reagan/Bush (always with the cooperative-votes of Senator Dole).

CLINTON'S FISCAL YEAR 1995 BUDGET

February 7, 1994: President Clinton sent his Fiscal Year *1995 Budget Message* to the Congress. He projected $1,518.3 billion total outlays with a deficit of $176.1 billion for FY'95. (See Appendix I for a reprint of the summary of Clinton's 1995 Budget.)

The dollar amount of the Federal debt (then exceeding $4.56 trillion) was not discussed.
Instead, the ability of the U.S. private sector to bear the debt interest burden was imputed to be related to some very speculative forecasts of *Gross Domestic Product (GDP)*

This was an innovation when compared with previous Federal budgets, and permitted an ingenious representation of Federal debt and net interest thereon *as a percent of GNP.* (*Clinton Budget* pages 42-43.)

See Table I-2, *Economic Assumptions* of the Clinton FY'95 Budget (Appendix I, hereto).

Note: The bottom-line cost of money (i.e., interest rates on the ever-increasing Federal debt) exceeds any other percent number on that table, including inflation as measured by the Consumer Price Index.

Author's opinion: The *GDP* methodology makes as little sense as if a mortgage lender were to consider only an applicant's annual income from sales of goods and services... without taking into account the applicant's net worth based on assets minus liabilities. The lender simply would not make or extend a mortgage loan based on such principles. Further, a lender would never make such a loan without a commitment to pay down principal plus interest on a preset schedule.
Leon Panetta, then Director of the Office of Management and Budget, headed the preparation and presentation of the FY'95 Budget.

March 11, 1994: Having made a few billion dollars of "adjustments," the House of Representatives cast its vote on the Clinton FY'95 budget. In a 223-175 roll call vote, there was a unanimous "no" vote by Republicans. (Source: *Congressional Record* 3/11/94, and New York Times 3/12/94).

March 25, 1994: The Senate voted to cut $26 billion over a period of five years from the Clinton FY'95 budget... much of which was cut from programs that are most important to the most vulnerable households in the United States. The Senate vote was 48 "yes" and 57 "no." The only Republican Senators voting to **not** cut the budget further were Mark O. Hatfield of Oregon and James M. Jeffords of Vermont.

The Budget then went to Joint Committees of the House and Senate, where it is being debated before coming back to the full House and Senate for a final vote later this year.
(Sources: *Congressional Record* 3/11/94 and 3/25/94 and New York Times 3/12/94 and 3/26/94)

As Will Rogers said, "We have the best politicians money can buy!"

STATE AND LOCAL DEBT

Although this is not the main subject of this book, it should be noted that the sum-total of state and local debt is $1.2 trillion. This is in addition, of course, to the present $4.6+ billions of Federal debt.

Of that $1.2 trillion amount, *American households* directly own $488 billion of municipal bonds, plus $414 billion indirectly via mutual funds and other investment vehicles.

(Sources: Securities and Exchange Commission, Special to New York Times, 3/10/94, and Treasury Department, *Gross Debt of State and Local Governments,* via Tax Foundation 1993, Table A18, p.20.)

U.S. NEGATIVE BALANCE OF TRADE IS PART OF THE PROBLEM

The United States trade deficit for goods and services soured, in February, 1994, to 9.71 billion...its worst level in six years. This was followed by $6.87 billion in March and $8.40 billion in April.

February's total imports of $50.1 billion included $8.8 billion American imports of foreign cars. Meanwhile, foreigners bought fewer U.S. made aircraft, computers and industrial engines.

(Sources: U.S. Department of Commerce, via new York Times, 3/16 and 3/20/94, and *Barron's Market Week*, 7/18/94.)

Author's comment: Annualized, the above could mean a trade deficit of $100 billion, or more, if the trend continues.

I am not a trade-isolationist, and I believe it is not good policy to impose taxes, embargoes, and boycotts on international trade for political purposes in peacetime.

But the trade-deficit subtracts from the Gross Domestic Product because it means that an increased part of American consumer demand is being satisfied by goods and services produced abroad. And not in the U.S.

It would be far more considerate of the need for more manufacturing jobs in the U.S. (and immensely helpful to the U.S. economy), if more of our citizens would "Buy American-Manufactured," when equivalent goods (as automobiles) are available.

> This would be an easier and more effective way to deal with Japan (where we ran a $59.3 billion deficit in 1993) than is our present ineffective and unenforceable diplomatic struggle over balance of trade with that country.

It must be recognized that a continuing net-outflow of money (due to a negative balance of trade), effectively diminishes the private sector's net worth and the national wealth, and increases the deficit and the U.S. national debt (because of the lost income taxes to the U.S. Treasury).

By the above means, we could quietly *shift* the unbalance of trade toward a more neutral position. Thus we would have more cash remaining in the United States to help reduce the Federal deficit.

The result would be three magnificent additional advantages:

1) Increase employment of U.S. workers.

2) Take millions of people off of unemployment roles and the costs associated therewith.

3) Provide more jobs yielding more personal income, which would provide billions of dollars or additional income taxes to the U.S. Treasury, which in turn would help to reduce the deficit and the debt.

NET WORTH OF THE PRIVATE SECTOR OF THE UNITED STATES

The source of the following data is The Federal Reserve Board, *Balance Sheets for the U.S. Economy 1945-1993, C.9, Table B.11*, p.7 et seq. dated 3/9/94, which is reproduced as Appendix II, hereto.

The **Balance sheets** summarize the tangible assets of the private sector of the United States, offset by all private sector liabilities. Reconciliation tables appear in the Balance Sheets.

Household net assets	13.1 trillion
Nonfinancial business net worth	6.0 trillion
Private financial institutions net assets	2.9 trillion

Private Sector Total Net Worth (Consolidated) $22.0 trillion

Note: In the FRB's Consolidated *Balance Sheets for the U.S. Economy* (above)... as is always done on balance sheets, big and small...every one person's (or entity's) debt or liability is another person's (or entity's) asset.

Note: We are *all* "private sector," incidentally, including politicians and public employees in their roles as taxpayers and voters, along with everyone else.

RATIO OF FEDERAL DEBT TO PRIVATE SECTOR NET WORTH

Author's comment:

From the foregoing, we can more clearly see the relative magnitude of the ever-increasing, snowballing, compounding, unpaid Federal debt.

Specifically, the Federal debt is already 21% of the entire private sector's net worth.

President Clinton's FY'95 additional deficit projections total $918.6 billions by the end of 1999. The projections contain no provisions for debt reduction and amortization. Thus, from the present 4.627 trillion debt (even if deficits remain as small as projected) this country is headed "ever-deeper in debt."

Further, the Federal Reserve Board's *Balance Sheets* show the private sector net worth as having grown at an average rate of 2% per year from 1989-1993. With the Federal debt simultaneously increasing at the average rate of more than 6% per year, anyone can easily see that the debt is over-running our private net worth by a rate of at least 4% per year (according to figures in the FY'95 budget, and the Federal Reserve Board's *Statistical Release*, 6/14/94).

This is, therefore, a terribly dangerous situation for this country... particularly so long as we have no plan to pay down the debt (even as a credit card company or home mortgage company would require.)

We desperately need a plan of action to start reducing the debt in 1995. At the same time, we must carry on our national life in a reasonable way.

DISTRIBUTION OF WEALTH IN THE UNITED STATES

At the end of 1993, there were 100 million households in the U.S.

The wealthiest 1/2% (or 500 thousand) households were estimated to have held 28.8% of the U.S. private sector *net worth*, compared to 24.3% six years earlier.

The next-wealthiest 1/2% of households were estimated to have held 8.3% of the U.S. private sector *net worth*, compared with 7.2% six years earlier.

Thus, (working from the $22.0 trillion private sector net worth statement, p. 33,) the combined top 1% (or 1 million households) are estimated to have had a total net worth of $8.2 trillion.

The wealthiest 1% of households are estimated to hold 79% of all public and private bonded debt assets, 62% of private business assets, and 45% of real estate assets other than principal residences.

Sources of above:

a) *1993 Green Book, Ways and Means Committee, U.S. House of Representatives,* pp. 1548-1562.

b) *Balance Sheets of the U.S. Economy 1945-1993,* Federal Reserve System, 3/9/94.

c) Board of Governors of the Federal Reserve System, *Federal Reserve Bulletin,* January 1992 Table No. 732, *Family Net Worth* (see Appendix III, hereto.

d) *Statistical Abstracts of the United States 1993.*

e) *Forbes,* October 18, 1993, *Forbes 400.*

f) U.S. Bureau of Census data, 1993.

These data are consolidated and plotted on the *Distribution of Wealth* graph on the following page.

DISTRIBUTION OF WEALTH IN THE UNITED STATES (Graph)

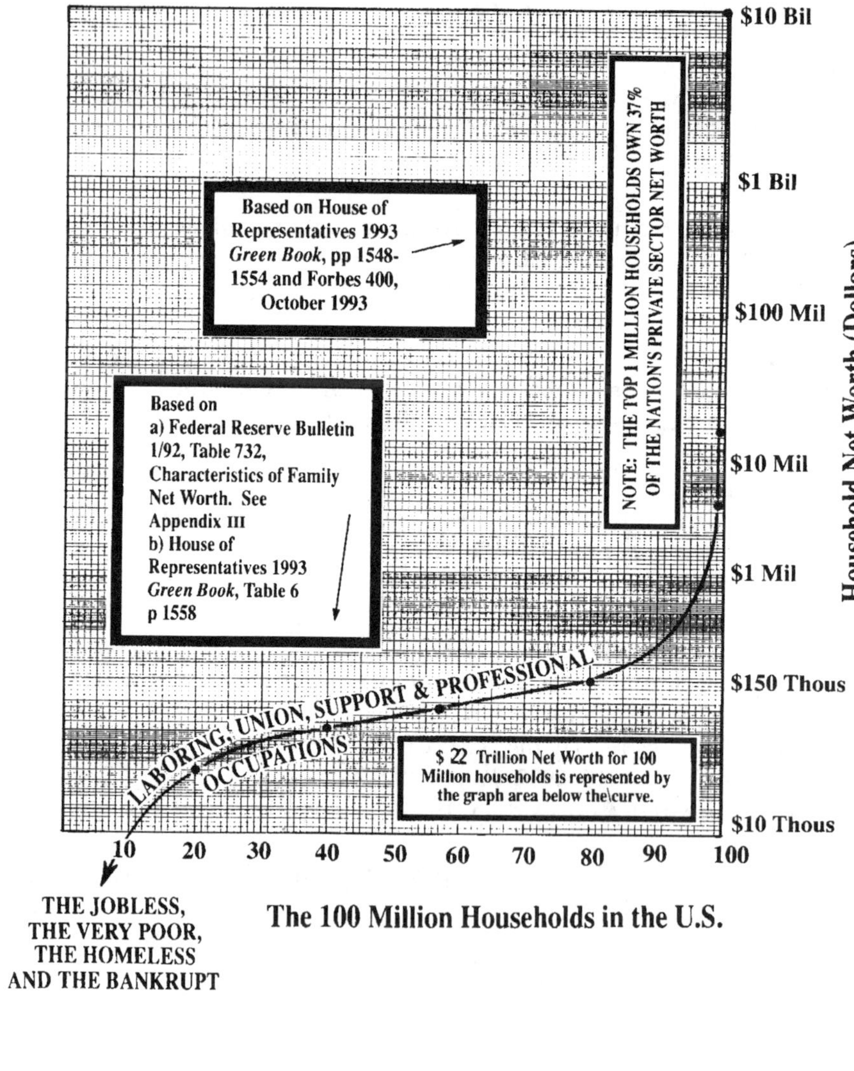

Author's comments:

The most shocking aspect of the wealth distribution data is the exceedingly-wide range of values from 20 million households with less than $30,000 net worth, and less than $10,000 annual income... to only one million households at the opposite end of the scale.

This disparity between the poor and the wealthy significantly widened during the Reagan/Bush years, as seen in the reproduced tables in Appendix III. See also feature article of Business Week, 8/15/94, *Inequality.: How The Gap Between Rich and Poor Hurts the Economy.*

Even more alarming are the revelations of the graph on the previous page, that nearly 80% (or 80 million U.S. households) have net worths less than $150,000 each. And 87% (or 87 million households) have net worths of less than $200,000 each.

It is a mathematical fact that, for any given amount of wealth, if principal and earnings are retained and continuously-reinvested, the accumulated-wealth compounds-upward, ever-increasingly, in a logarithmic manner.

Therefore, I have used so-called "semi-log" graph paper to demonstrate distribution of wealth in the graph on the page 36.

The integral area under any portion of the graph represents the whole amount of dollars involved for that portion of the graph...down to a single household.

And the integral area under the entire curve accurately represents the $22.0 trillion total net worth of the private sector.

A note of caution is in order regarding interpretation of the Distribution of Wealth Graph: The use of *semi-log* graph paper (on which to plot the household net worth data) tends to obscure the dollar magnitudes as we usually think of them when we see them plotted to a linear scale.

On the Distribution of Wealth graph , $100,000 is approximately one inch. At the top of the right hand side of the graph are household net worths up to $10 billion.

If $10 billion were plotted on a more usual linear scale, the height of the curve would be over 800 feet.

FEDERAL INCOME TAXES

Roosevelt, Truman and Eisenhower kept income taxes high to maintain the national-project of World War II, and its expensive post-war phase, without increasing deficits and running-up significant Federal debt. (See Table, p. 18.)

Author's Comments:

We are now faced with a different kind of threat ...*national bankruptcy*... which must become a project of a different kind, of national scope, for which we must increase taxes that have long been too low to sustain national programs.

The book: *America: Who Really Pays the Taxes?*, by Pulitzer Prize winners Donald J. Barlett and James B. Steele (published by Simon and Schuster, 1994), aptly describes the inequities in the U.S. income tax system which have provided (and continue to provide) many tax loopholes, allowances, perquisites and special giveaways to the influential and the wealthy. I urge you to read it (Paperback $9.95).

These income tax benefits (which amount to very large *entitlements* to the wealthy) simply are not available to the households depicted at the lower end of the Distribution of Wealth Curve, p. 36.

Unlike several other prominent authors from 1992-1994 who propose "no increase in taxes"... Barlett and Steele do make several constructive proposals which Congress should consider to create a much more progressive tax structure, by eliminating preferential inequities, increasing taxes on very wealthy, and making considerable structural changes in income tax formulas (see B&S, pp. 338-340). They recommend tax increases for the wealthy, along with a few decreases for the less-wealthy, which would bring large amounts of money into the Treasury and would certainly decrease the annual deficits.

However, like other recent authors, Barlett and Steele propose to use income tax restructuring only to reduce the Federal Deficits.

They never get around to mentioning the Federal Debt.

FEDERAL ESTATE TAXES

The Federal Estate Tax is clearly non-progressive, and enormously favors the already-wealthy.

Exemplary, are the facts that...

> *a $25,000 estate* is incrementally taxed at 22%;
> *a $250,000 estate* is incrementally taxed at 34%;
> *a $2.5 million estate* is incrementally taxed at only 53%;
> *a $3 million estate,* and all larger estates are incrementally taxed at only 55%.
> (Source: Internal Revenue Service, *Gift and Estate Tax Rate Tables , 1992.*)

It is seen from the above table that the incremental-tax percentages from 22% to 55% (representing a multiple of only 2.5) in no way matches the unchanging non-progressive 55% tax assessments on estates from $3 million... to $30 million... to $3 billion or higher.

To further demonstrate how ridiculously low the Estate and Gift Tax formulas are for the wealthy:

This set of taxes brought in only $82 billion into the Treasury during the past seven years.

> That is only 1.1% of all Federal tax receipts during those same years!

(Source: Treasury Department and Office of Management and Budget, *Federal Receipts by Source Fiscal Years 1987-1993,* via Tax Foundation, 1993, Table C3, p.85.)

Author's opinion: The combined non-progressive Federal Estate and Gift Tax formulas of the United States are an "illusion" and a fraud on the country as a whole.

Both Estate Tax and Income Tax formulas are exceedingly nonprogressive and inequitable. That's where the real "smoke and mirrors" are, Senator Dole!

Author's recommendation: In exchange for that negligible 1.1% of total tax receipts from Gift and Estate Taxes brought into the Treasury, annually... Simply *abolish* those taxes. And replace them by a Net Worth Tax as proposed herein.

AUTHOR'S OBSERVATIONS

Low income taxes and low capital gain taxes, along with low estate taxes have reinforced each other to bring-about the fastest, greatest upward migration of wealth in the history of the United States. The result is that as the rich have definitely become richer, while the poor have definitely become poorer (see Appendix III).

The wealthy made excellent investment-use of those interest-free $ billions on which they were *not* required to pay income taxes from 1970-1992.

Using that no-cost money, the wealthy invested and re-invested in high-potential rapid growth companies and lucrative high-yielding tax-exempt municipal bonds. Thus, they compounded their net worths, annually.

The wealthy have also taken enormous advantage of special income tax exemptions via countless tax gimmicks which caused greatly diminished income to the Treasury over the years. An all-encompassing Net Worth Tax would recoup many of those lost dollars in the future, and would counteract such inequities in the future, pending changes in income tax and estate tax laws.

On the other hand, there is no doubt that many very-wealthy people earned their fortunes by way of great initiative, enterprise and entrepreneurship.

The vignettes in Forbes 400 re-tell the story each October. These people have sparked whole new industries since World War II. They have created millions of jobs and by-and-large done enormous good for this country.

Books by other authors will honor them.

The purpose of <u>this</u> book is to trigger political action toward a solution to the Federal debt and the problems it has created.

FUNCTIONAL ILLITERACY IN THE UNITED STATES

Nearly half of the 191 million adults in the United States are deemed to be not-proficient-enough in reading, writing and arithmetic to function well in their jobs and in society as a whole.

(Source: *Literacy Report* dated 9/8/93 by U.S. Department of Education collaboration with U.S. Department of Labor).

The reasons for this sad state of affairs are many, of course, ranging from individuals' severe mental and emotional handicaps, to lack of self-motivation and drive...to insufficient funding from the Federal Government to state and local governments...due, in turn, to the ever-increasing Federal deficit...due to the cost of financing the Federal debt.

For whatever the combined reasons, the problem of functional illiteracy in the United States is tremendous, and is the direct cause of many other societal problems, particularly among the unemployed and the poor.

POVERTY AND MISERY IN THE UNITED STATES... THE COLD, HARD FACTS:

28 million people live in households that are below the poverty line... of which 13.9 million are children.

> The poverty level is a yardstick based on the amount of money necessary to purchase the lowest cost "nutritionally adequate" diet under the current *Thrifty Food Plan* of the U.S. Agriculture Dept. that price tag is multiplied by 3 to produce a poverty threshold (which includes the cost of diet, plus twice that amount to purchase other goods and service, including clothing, rents and transportation. Adjustments are made for size of household.

27.6 million people live in households which receive food stamps from the U.S. Department of Agriculture.

(Source: *Consolidated Report on Poverty*, 10/4/93, U.S. Department of Labor, Bureau of Labor Statistics in cooperation with U.S. Department of Health and Human Services and U.S. Department of Commerce, Bureau of Census).

At the end of June, 1994, 130 million people were available in the work force, of which

7.8 million, or 6%, were unemployed, and

5.0 million were underemployed, (i.e. those who would like to find work, but who can't find adequate jobs), and

1.7 million people were working below the federal minimum wage of $4.25/hour, and

2.5 million people were working at the minimum wage of 4.25 per hour.

> (Note: Senator Dole and his Republican followers have consistently blocked increasing the minimum wage)

(Source: Department of Labor, Bureau of Labor Statistics, 4/29/94 and 6/30/94.)

THE HOMELESS are a floating population of at least 600,000 people any given night. Some of them occupy up to 275,000 beds in emergency shelters. (Source: Based on Bush Administration data, Newsweek 4/6/92, p. 29).

Due to changes in federal funding policies during the Reagan/Bush years, a disproportionate number of the homeless were driven onto the streets because of mental illness and substance abuse. From then, they were not provided treatment as may have been necessary in treatment centers. Also, federally funded housing fundng was cut, as was funding to the States for the unmet medical needs of the homeless.

A report being prepared for President Clinton estimates that as many as 7 million Americans were homeless at some point in the late 1980s. (New York Times, 2/17/94)... A number considered too high by a number of independent researchers.

The U.S. Conference of Mayors in 1994 has called on the Federal Government to help with the problem of the homeless of whom 43% are families, and 21% are veterans. Thirty percent of those people seeking emergency food are unemployed.

Author's note: Certainly, there is a wide disparity of statistics in re the homeless. The actual numbers probably lie somewhere in between.

Whatever the data (the dollars, or the numerical statistics), however, the measure of human misery among the homeless is another sad matter that must be addressed (given the budget-power to do so).

AID TO FAMILIES WITH DEPENDENT CHILDREN (AFDC)

The following facts (Source: *New York Times*, 3/19/94) should help to put into focus many misconceptions about this unfortunate segment of our society.

At the end of 1993, an average of 4.9 million households per month were receiving AFDC aid. Only 9% of those households had a father in the home. The total number of children in those households was 9.5 million, for an average number of children per household at 1.9.

38.4% of households receiving AFDC aid are white families.

40.1% of households receiving AFDC aid are black families.

15.9% of households receiving AFDC aid are Hispanic families.

The total cost of programs in 1993 was $23 billion for the 4.9 million AFDC households.

The median length of time on AFDC assistance is 25 months.

62% of AFDC families have been on the rolls for less than 3 years

> 50% were less than 2 years.
> 32% were less than 1 year.

80% of AFDC families have only one child under 12 years of age.

57% of AFDC families have only one child under 6 years of age.

35% of AFDC families have only one child under 3 years of age.

"ENTITLEMENT PROGRAMS"

The Clinton Fiscal Year 1995 Budget called for the following so called "entitlement program" costs through 1999, as follows:

	FY'95	**FY'99**
Social Security Benefits (already owned by beneficiaries)	$335 billions	$411
Federal Retirement Benefits (already owned beneficiaries)	65	79
Medicare	153	215
Medicaid	96	101
Unemployment Benefits	23	25
Family Support Benefits (including food stamps)	97	124
Debt Interest Cost	**213**	**255**

Thus it is seen that the interest cost on the debt exceeds, by far, the cost of any of the so-called "entitlement programs," except Social Security.

WASTED RESOURCES

Certainly, I am against waste of all kinds which increases the cost of government. And waste should be reduced or eliminated wherever possible. But a lot depends on your definition of "wasted" time and money!

I would establish the following priorities:

a) We should stop *wasting* kids and adults due to lack of adequate education, nutrition, and health care.

b) We should concentrate on not-wasting *natural resources.* Programs should be intensified to recover natural resources by encouraging the establishment with huge job-providing waste-recovery programs in the private sector.

c) There is far too much *time* wasted by both the private and public sectors due to paper work and reporting requirements for governmental purposes. The problem is particularly acute in re health care and represents far too large a percentage of health care costs. Ditto, the required filling out of too many government forms, particularly tax forms (notwithstanding the so-called "Reduction in Paperwork Act").

d) *Underutilized U.S. Government-owned facilities and lands* should be considered for sale to the private sector, thus reducing government-overhead and bringing cash into the Treasury. However, the total physical assets of the U.S. at the end of 1992 were valued at only $1.9 trillion (source: Office of Management and Budget via Tax Foundation *Table C5 Federal Assets and Liabilities*).

   But, only a part of those would be available for sale, and only a few private-sector buyers might be interested. So those would not represent a lot of cash to pay the debt.

e) *More U.S. Government-provided services* should be considered to be contracted to the private sector. This would provide more taxable income to the Treasury, and, likely, afford higher efficiencies.

f) Congress should consider quasi-privatization of additional programs such as the U.S. Postal Service and Amtrak. Air Traffic Control would be among the possibilities.

PART II
THE SOLUTION

AMORTIZE THE FEDERAL DEBT

A NET WORTH TAX STARTING IN 1995

IS OUR NATION'S

ONLY WAY OUT

CONGRESSIONAL ACTION IS NEEDED NOW

There is no question that Congress must act in 1994 or early 1995, to amortize the Federal debt to head off national bankruptcy.

Congress must pass a *Net Worth Tax Law,* to become effective 1/1/95 to bring funds into the Treasury to reduce the Federal debt.

This is the only remaining, reasonable way to balance the budget.

And save the country from bankruptcy.

Treasury collections on the Net Worth Tax would not actually begin until April 15, 1995 at the earliest (coincident with payment of 1994 income taxes).

The obtainable results are shown on the Debt Amortization Tables, which are detailed on Appendix IV, and summarized on pages 51, 52 and 53.

Because time is of the essence, upon introduction of this subject for debate, Congress should immediately invoke cloture rules to prevent lengthy filibusters during this highly-important legislative process.

Note: The U.S. Supreme Court decided, May, 1994, that Congress's budgetary responsibility under the Constitution gives Congress and the IRS the power to collect taxes retroactively.

NET WORTH TRUST FUND TO BE ESTABLISHED

To protect Net Worth Tax funds from misappropriation, Congress should establish a sacrosanct *Net Worth Tax Trust Fund* to be governed by an independent *private-sector* Board of Trustees whose charter is two fold:

1) *Provide oversight* over the receipt of all Net Worth Taxes coming into the Treasury.

2) *See-to-it* that the *Trust Fund* is used only for the purpose of paying-down the national debt according to established priorities:

    a) *Pay-back* previous U.S. Government borrowings from other Trust Funds (Social Security Trust Fund being first);

    b) *Pay-back* all U.S. borrowings from U.S. citizens (via "calls" or "buy-backs" of U.S. Bonds, Notes and Bills);

    c) *Pay all foreign-debts outstanding*, by repurchase of all U.S. Bonds, Notes and Bills held by foreign owners.

The expected result: *Once the debt is gone, and if income taxes are maintained at sufficiently-high-levels to support program-costs, the budget can be balanced.*

DEBT AMORTIZATION VIA NET WORTH TAXES TO BE COLLECTED

Three alternatives, or plans, appear in the following proposed debt-amortization schedules:

Plan A is to amortize the Federal debt in six years, from 1995 to 2000, according to the Net Worth Tax Schedule, Appendix IV-A.

Plan B is to amortize the debt in ten years, from 1995 to 2003, at a Net Worth Tax Rate 75% of that used in Plan A, but according to the Net Worth Tax Schedule, Appendix IV-B.

Plan C is to amortize the debt in 18 years, from 1995 to 2011, at a Net Worth Tax Rate 50% of that used in Plan A, according to the Net Worth Tax Schedule, Appendix IV-C.

All three plans and tables are computed at a compounding rate of only 7.5% per year cost to the U.S. Treasury. If interest rates increase above 7.5%, all elements on these tables will increase exponentially, including dollars and the number of years for debt amortization.

The summary amortization tables for **Plans A, B** and **C** appear on the following three pages, 51, 52 and 53.

AMORTIZATION PLAN A - 6 YEARS

(For details, see Appendix IV-A)

Date	National Debt remaining from previous year	Plus Interest @ 7.5% to next year	Minus NW Taxes received by Treasury next year	Amortized Debt Balance
	$ Billions	$ Billions	$ Billions	$ Billions
4/14/94	4,562	342	1,725 4/15/95	3,179
4/14/95	3,179	238	1,238 4/15/96	2,180
4/14/96	2,180	163	900 4/15/97	1,444
4/14/97	1,444	108	720 4/15/98	832
4/14/98	832	62	612 4/15/99	282
4/14/99	282	21	520	–217
Total Interest Cost Plan A		**$ 936 billion**		

AMORTIZATION PLAN B - 10 YEARS

Based on 75% of maximum proposed amortization rate of Plan A.
(For details, see Appendix IV-B)

Date	National Debt remaining from previous year	Plus Interest @ 7.5% to next year	Minus NW Taxes received by Treasury next year	Amortized Debt Balance
	$ Billions	$ Billions	$ Billions	$ Billions
4/14/94	4,562	342	1,207	3,697
			4/15/95	
4/14/95	3,697	277	969	3,005
			4/15/96	
4/14/96	3,005	225	761	2,469
			4/15/97	
4/14/97	2,469	185	645	2,009
			4/15/98	
4/14/98	2,009	151	570	1,590
			4/15/99	
4/14/99	1,590	119	505	1,205
			4/15/00	
4/14/00	1,205	90	453	842
			4/15/01	
4/14/01	842	63	444	460
			4/15/02	
4/14/02	460	35	406	89
			4/15/03	
4/14/03	89	7	427	–332
Total Interest Cost Plan B		**$ 1,495 billion**		

AMORTIZATION PLAN C - 18 YEARS

Based on 50% of maximum proposed amortization rate of Plan A.
(For details, see Appendix IV-C)

Date	National Debt remaining from previous year	Plus Interest @ 7.5% to next year	Minus NW Taxes received by Treasury next year	Amortized Debt Balance
	$ Billions	$ Billions	$ Billions	$ Billions
4/14/94	4,562	342	862	4,042
4/14/95	4,042	303	4/15/95 738	3,606
4/14/96	3,606	270	4/15/96 624	3,253
4/14/97	3,253	244	4/15/97 539	2,958
4/14/98	2,958	222	4/15/98 487	2,693
4/14/99	2,693	202	4/15/99 434	2,461
4/14/00	2,461	185	4/15/00 395	2,251
4/14/01	2,251	169	4/15/01 370	2,049
4/14/02	2,049	154	4/15/02 341	1,862
4/14/03	1,862	140	4/15/03 343	1,658
4/14/04	1,658	124	4/15/04 320	1,463
4/14/05	1,463	110	4/15/05 326	1,246
4/14/06	1,246	93	4/15/06 305	1,035
4/14/07	1,035	78	4/15/07 285	827
4/14/08	827	62	4/15/08 300	590
4/14/09	590	44	4/15/09 281	353
4/14/10	353	26	4/15/10 265	114
4/14/11	114	9	4/15/11 247	–124

Total Interest Cost Plan C **$ 2,230 billion**

HOW THE NET WORTH TAX SYSTEM WOULD WORK FOR YOU

From your personal point of view the proposed Net Worth Tax System would work as follows:

1) Find the point where your household net worth lies on the Distribution of Wealth Curve, appearing page 36 . You will then see where you personally are with respect to 100 million other households in the United States.

2) If your present household net worth is less than $150,000 at the end of any given year, you would not be required to pay a Net Worth Tax for that year.

   See Appendix IV, Plan B, for exemplary rates for the 10-year Federal Debt Amortization Plan:

3) Households having net worths from $150,000 to $200,000 would be required to pay at the rate of 0.7% per year for as many years as they remain in that bracket.

4) Households having net worths from $200,000 to $600,000 would be required to pay at the rate of 1.4% per year for as many years as they remain in that bracket.

5) Households having net worths of $800 thousand to $1.5 million would be required to pay at the rate of 2.8% per year for as many years as they remain in that bracket.

6) Households having net worths of $135 million to $185 million would be required to pay at the rate of 21.0% per year for as many years as they remain in that bracket... etc.

TO MY FELLOW AMERICANS:

The Net Worth Tax formula is admittedly stiff for the wealthy. But *it is also equitable.* No one can possibly go broke from paying this tax.

"Even after paying their fair share, the wealthy will still have more on their plates than they can possibly eat."

We have already allowed ourselves too long to recognize how deeply in debt we have become.

As it has always been, digging one's self out of deep debt is like trying to dig one's way out of a deep hole in the sand. With every shovel full thrown out, some sand slides back into the hole. *Unless we use very-large shovels-full and work as fast as we can, we will never get out of the hole.*

So, I have proposed higher net worth tax rates than I would have liked. But there is no alternative.

After all, this matter of paying the debt is only taking money out of one set of pockets and paying it into another pocket (the U.S. Treasury). When this is completed, we will have a long-lived, healthy, bankrupt-proof nation in which business-opportunities will be greater than ever before.

We can only hope that the Federal Reserve Bank can continue to hold interest at low rates (not exceeding a weighted average of 7.5%) while we work to achieve the needed results.

In the first eight months of 1994 the brakes have already started to slip. The Federal Reserve Bank has increased short term interest rates five times for a total of 1 3/4%.

As a result, major banks have raised the prime rate they charge their most-favored and reliable customers from 6.0% up to 7.75% (the highest increase in many years). This means we will have higher business and consumer expenses and higher interest rates on millions of small business loans, home mortgages, and credit card loans that are linked to the prime rate. This is real inflation.

Meanwhile, stock and bond markets, where so many people's savings are invested, have fallen and have become increasingly jittery.

The underlying reason, of course, is that the Federal debt has gotten out of control. And the FY'95 Federal Budget shows large deficits (and therefore ever-larger debt) for the balance of this century.

WHO WOULD BE REQUIRED TO FILE AND PAY NET WORTH TAXES

The following entities would be required to file Net Worth Tax declarations, annually:

* All households, individuals or entities who are required to file income tax returns.

* All households, individuals or entities having net worths in excess of $50,000 would be required to *file.*

* All fiduciaries, trustees and guardians in re the net assets of each account under their management, including (but not limited to) beneficial trusts, revocable trusts, blind trusts, guardianships, etc.

(Net Worth Taxes would be paid by trustees or guardians out of the *principal amounts* of said accounts.)

* Generally, all nonprofit institutions and ventures *having income-tax-exempt status* would be exempt from paying net worth taxes, but they would be required to *file.*

* *Private* clubs, associations and ventures would be taxed according to the present as was market value of their assets minus liabilities.

ITEMS TO BE DECLARED FOR NET WORTH TAXES

To be *declared* would be all items set forth in Appendix V.

To simplify reporting of assets and liabilities, at the election of the taxpayer, an outside appraiser or tax accountant could be used to estimate the valuation of assets and liabilities. Real estate valuations could be the same as local tax statements show.

Net worth reportings would be similar to those presently used for estate tax reportings. Members of Congress would be held to the same standards.

Short forms would be used for households whose net worths are less than $150,000. They would require relatively few minutes to complete.

PROCEDURES FOR FILING AND PAYING NET WORTH TAXES

If a Net Worth Tax Law is passed to become effective January 1, 1995, this would give many people time to adjust their gifting and investment programs during 1995.

Congress could stipulate that the Net Worth Tax program would continue in effect until the national debt is reduced to zero.

Net Worth Tax filings and payments would be made simultaneously with income tax returns (starting April 15, 1995).

A ten year time-frame (Plan B) would allow any and all entities sufficient time to smoothly adjust their portfolios, without flooding and depressing the markets by too many sales of any particular type of asset in any single year.

The tax-estimating and installment-payment features used for Net Worth Taxes would be similar to those used for income taxes.

Some entities may find it necessary to sell some assets (at a capital gain or loss) to make their Net Worth Tax payments as they become due.

Several possibilities exist:

1) Because the Federal Debt is primarily represented by private ownership of U.S. bonds, notes and bills by U.S. citizens... Congress should establish that a taxpayer-entity owning such securities could elect to pay its Net Worth Tax (in total or in part) in any year, by *direct redemption* by the U.S. Treasury of those securities at full market value, as payment for the tax.

   This would avoid the need that the taxpaying entity might have to sell those bonds, bills and notes via a secondary market at a lower net price.

2) If an entity must sell a unitized-asset (as a large building), then (for income tax purposes) provisions would be made to help "ease the pain" when payments are due, as follows:

   a) If the cash received is used within 6 months to pay incremental Net Worth Taxes, then capital gains (if any) would be forgiven from income taxes, and would not be taxed as capital gains.

b) Net capital losses incurred for the specific purpose of paying Net Worth Taxes would be deductible from gross income, for income tax purposes.

3) *Alternatively,* if a Net Worth Taxable entity should opt to sell an asset (or a set of assets) in anticipation of a *future* Net Worth Tax payment, then...

a) The taxable-entity would (in advance) declare as was to the Internal Revenue Service.

b) Upon receiving payment from the sale, the taxable-entity would make an advance payment to the Treasury in the amount of the Net Worth Taxes due for "x" years ahead.

c) The Treasury would treat the advance payment and as if it was the purchase of a short term Treasury Note. And would pay interest to the entity at the going rate for the balance of the term.

d) For income tax purposes, the interest earned would be treated as is interest earned by the entity from any other U.S. Government obligation(s).

ENFORCEMENT AND PENALTIES

Collection and enforcement would be responsibility of the Internal Revenue Service.

Author's suggestion: Penalties of 2 or 3 times the Net Worth Taxes due would probably deter most temptations to misrepresent the facts. Criminal penalties, where indicated, would be applied as in extreme cases of income tax fraud.

Author's belief: My guess is that the very presence of a net worth tax would bring to light and expose a vast spectrum of con artists, loan sharks, quacks, chiselers, cheats, swindlers, drug pushers, pimps, and other fraudulent and illegal enterprises that would not otherwise be discovered by income tax laws, because of their previous failures to file income tax returns.

> Also, *social security scofflaws* who fail to file and pay social security benefits for their "nannies" and often-underpaid employees.

With the *teeth* that a net worth tax enforcement law would have, many non-payers of taxes could be detected and brought to justice and their illegal practices terminated, and their unethical enterprises could be shut down.

LOW NET WORTH HOUSEHOLDS

The Distribution of Wealth graph which appears p. 36, shows that approximately 80 million, or 80%, of all households in the U.S. have net worths less than $150,000 each. For those households this amount represents primarily their investments in their homes, small businesses (if any), and a few thousands of dollars in savings and investments.

Therefore, I recommend omitting them from payment of the Net Worth Taxes even though they would be required to <u>file</u> Net Worth Tax Declarations, yearly.

> For these households, $150,000 would act as baseline-protection for both their working and retirement years, in addition to whatever retirement income they have from Social Security, Investment Retirement Accounts (IRAs), Employee Stock Option Plans (ESOPs), KEOGH Accounts, 401(k) plans, etc..

Author's Opinion: Overall, *considerable economic advantage* will come from this exemption for the least wealthy because, in addition to the *financial security* provided, these households will have more spending money to put back into the economy.

> This spending will, in turn, create additional income and benefits to the entire economy because greater income and <u>taxable profits</u> will accrue to vendors of goods and services sold to the low net worth households.

NET WORTH TAXES ON BUSINESS ENTERPRISES TO BE EXEMPTED

All business enterprises, including family ventures, proprietorships, general and/or limited partnerships, associations, public or private companies (incorporated or not-incorporated, domestic and/or foreign), joint ventures, ad hoc "arrangements" and illegal situations would be required to file Net Worth Tax Returns, annually.

> It would be up to Congress to decide whether or not to require Net Worth Taxes to be paid by those entities.

Author's Recommendations: *Profits* of business enterprises would continue to be subject to income taxes. Therefore, I propose that Congress not require Net Worth Taxes to be paid by business enterprises (although they should be required to file).

AUTHOR'S COMMENTS

Many millions of high income households enjoyed considerable advantages (due to low income taxes) during those low tax years 1970-92. Therefore, payments of Net Worth Taxes to reduce the National Debt should be a task in which they should be glad to participate.

Special note: It would not be realistic to require that the *1 million top-most wealthy-households together* (having combined net worth of $8.2 trillion at the end of 1993) be required to raise the total amount to pay the debt within the time-frame available.

I believe, however, that it would be in the best interests of the most-wealthy to help pay down the Federal Debt in the shortest possible number of years.

ADVANTAGES TO STARTING A DEBT AMORTIZATION PROGRAM IN 1995

It is seen that the Net Worth Tax program herein proposed is not a "socialist" attempt to redistribute the wealth, because this program does not take-away from the wealthy and give to the poor.

In addition to its other advantages, this program will simply create a more-level playing field so that (when all the pot-holes are filled-in) *all* citizens will increasingly prosper, as their enterprises (or their employer's enterprises) prosper even more.

After all the dust has settled, with increased economic activity, the wealthy, by their wits, will soon recover most of what they paid-out in Net Worth Taxes. That is the nature of the dynamism of entrepreneurially wealthy people.

Simultaneously, as the whole nation prospers, the working majority will have a better chance to improve their overall financial situations during their working years.

If we start a debt amortization program in 1995...

Instead of wasting the projected $213 to $255 billion on debt-interest each year, we could start spending some of that money in the private sector on health, education, and other needed societal programs.

We could pay back the $400 billion stolen from the Social Security Trust fund during the Reagan/Bush years, works were continuing to be borrowed under Clinton.

We could initiate more federal spending programs to put people back to work repairing dikes, bridges, roads, and programs benefiting the environment, etc. Those people could then better-survive and start paying income taxes.

If we start a debt reduction program in 1995...

We could head off the danger of runaway inflation that could be triggered due to not-enough money being available to the private sector to produce sufficient goods and commodities to meet demands.

The Net Worth Tax would certainly be a *kinder* control to inflation than raising interest rates, because higher interest rates would act to increase the costs of everything we buy, and would hurt profits throughout the economy (except for banks and money lenders).

If we start a debt amortization program in 1995...

We could avoid the risk of a financial panic due to money-worries such as occurred in the United States in 1929.

If we start a debt amortization program in 1995...

We would diminish fears for the future that are now causing so many business managers to lay off so many employees.

Therefore, entrepreneurs and their financial backers would be willing to risk more investments for the future... thus guaranteeing a brighter economy for the United States.

The wealthy would benefit due to more-profitable businesses, therefore...

More jobs would be created at higher incomes.

More jobs, in turn, would generate more income taxes to help finance U.S. and State governments.

In short, we would enter a gigantic positive-feedback loop replacing the potentially-devastating downward-spiraling Federal debt situation we are in today.

INTERNATIONALLY

If we start a debt amortization program in 1995...

We would gain advantage by calming fears in the International Banking Community, which is alarmed by the United States' increasing budget-deficits and increasing debt. (And is the major reason for the declining value of the dollar).

Respect for the United States would increase because we would be a strengthened country. The world would know that the U.S. would be able to do many things it cannot now do because of budget limitations due to the debt.

Because the U.S. dollar is the "currency of choice" around the world, a stabilized U.S. dollar would help to stabilize the world economy.

Conversely, a bankrupt United States could cause worldwide problems of unknown magnitude.

NATURAL DISASTERS

If we start a debt amortization program in 1995...

***Reserve funds** could be established* to provide (in advance) for quicker relief in natural disasters including earthquakes, floods, hurricanes, fires, and winter storms. And the tremendous costs of such programs needn't await costly, time-consuming Congressional debates to go "off-budget,"as occurred in 1993/1994.

We *know* such disasters are going to happen. So why wait to fund them?

ON A PERSONAL LEVEL

If we start a debt amortization program in 1995...

Consider how many people, including you, would just plain feel better and sleep better knowing that a program is in place to balance the budget and eliminate the Federal debt. Thus avoiding national bankruptcy, and with it, millions of personal and business bankruptcies.

Having more opportunities to succeed would cause many people to feel better about themselves. Thus they would act less destructively toward themselves, their families and society in general. They would also have less feelings of psychological depression.

Gifting by individuals (to tax-exempt organizations as schools, colleges, libraries, hospitals, artistic institutions, etc.) would increase as people unload large chunks of their net worth to allow them to leap into lower tax brackets and minimize their Net Worth Taxes.

CONCLUSION:

We already have an almost infinite gap between the "have-nots" and the "haves"... the unemployed and the employed... the sick and the well.

The 1992 civil riots in Los Angeles should be a warning that if the disparities are allowed to grow (both in values and in numbers of people) the U.S. could be heading toward conditions of civil unrest such as triggered the people's revolt in France in 1778, and the Russian Revolution in 1917.

Those were followed by similarly-induced revolutions in Spain from 1923-1936.

Similar unrest occurred in Brazil, caused by an unbalanced economic and political situation and extremely high inflation during the years 1974-1976.

How many warnings and examples does the United States need?

MOST IMPORTANTLY...

It would be totally unconscionable that this nation's children and grandchildren should be burdened with this intolerably-crushing debt created by our generation, during our lifetimes.

Think about it!

ALTERNATIVES TO DEBT REDUCTION

a) **Do nothing. And let the whole country (private and public sectors together) become bankrupt before the world.**

b) **Devalue the dollar** by having Treasury print more dollars to "pay" the debt.

This is what happened to Brazil, and this would be the worst possible solution. By this approach we would only be kidding ourselves because every 20% of newly minted money would cause each existing dollar to be worth 20% less.

Thus, the purchasing value of all personal savings and pensions would devastatingly decrease.

That could lead to financial panic and skyrocketing inflation as in the case of post World War I Germany.

c) **Wait for interest rates to escalate even more.**

Then the economy will deteriorate and, even worse, it will become impossible to play catch-up ball to reduce the Federal debt.

d) **The best alternative is to resolve and commit to debt-amortization along the lines of**

Plan A...6 years (p. 51 and Appendix IV-A) or
Plan B...10 years (p. 52 and Appendix IV-B) or
Plan C...18 years (p. 53 and appendix IV-C).

Plan A would allow us to get back on the track fastest and most assuredly in order to prevent national bankruptcy... And save $0.5 trillion to $1.2 trillions of dollars of interest costs, compared to **plans B** or **C**.

TRICKLEDOWN, BUBBLEUP, RECIRCULATION & POTBOILING

My conception of "trickledown" as it should be practiced is diametrically-opposite from that of Nixon, Reagan, and Bush, and their conferees.

> *Their* Keyensian view was that the money in the hands of the wealthy (due to low taxes) would "trickle-down" to stimulate the economy as a whole, to a sufficient extent that the taxed-profits generated thereby would zero-out the deficit.

The record shows that it just didn't work out as they hoped it would!

But Reagan cut taxes again in 1987, and the deficit and debt accelerated.

In contrast, *I believe* that trickledown cash from the Federal Government to even the non-wealthy provides the best-possible stimulus for growth of the economy.

Example: Federal money paid out to so-called "entitlement programs" to provide such as AFDC assistance to needy families, etc., is *immediately* spent to buy food and clothing. And is not wasted money.

> This kind of cash flow triggers a wide spectrum of purchases of products and services from many other sources.

The immediate result: All vendors, and their vendors and employees, would pay corporate and personal income taxes on their profits. Thus, there would be an immediate up-flow of tax-income into the Treasury.

Under this trickledown concept, Congress could authorize an increase of federally-funded infrastructure-projects (highways, bridges, flood control, etc.). This, too, is not wasted money.

> Think of the thousands and thousands of *jobs* these projects have created in the past (now being sharply curtailed or canceled by Congress because of budget constraints). And think again of the up-flow of income taxes into the Treasury that could result from such jobs.

From this same standpoint, putting more police on the streets for crime prevention is not wasted money, and would make great economic sense in addition to saving many lives and much property.

Under my trickledown concept, Congress could pass laws that would, in effect, order Treasury to release money into many diverse programs (including the funding of advanced research projects, such as those of NASA, high-energy accelerators for advanced research, astronomical telescopes and space stations, etc.), without "wasting" money.

> (Incidentally, research and development expenditures do not cause cash to leave this country. Those expenditures immediately trickle-down and recirculate into the U.S. private sector ...continuing to generate new income and income taxes to be collected by the Treasury.)

> *Conclusion of Fact: In this sense, trickledown, bubbleup, recirculation and potboiling together comprise a real win-win opportunity for the economy of the United States. And are not "wasted" money.*

Of course, *Congress knows* that there is not enough money in the budget to pay for all those beneficial activities.

The simple reason is: Congress's first priority must be to pay the projected $213 to $255 billions of annually increasing interest on the Federal debt from 1995 to 1999. (Source: Clinton Proposed Budget of the United States Government FY'95. See Appendix I, hereto.)

So, hundreds of needed programs including health care and education remain inadequately funded. And continue to swing in the wind.

OBJECTIONS AND ANSWERS TO OBJECTIONS

A number of people may object to certain aspects of this debt-amortization proposal. For example:

Objection: "Congress always spends too much on entitlement programs..." (meaning..."for the undeserving poor and the disadvantaged...").

Answers: With our representative form of government, that depends on the three (and only three) people you send to Washington from your State and District (two Senators and one Representative to the House of Representatives). Each State and District sends its own.

Being, then, on the Federal payroll...while they *should* act as if they are responsible for this country as a whole... too often they do not.

From Fiscal Years 1981 (Reagan) through 1993 (Bush), the Federal Debt increased by 449% (from $1,004 up to $4,411 billion). Congress went along.

Meanwhile, all Federal "entitlements" increased by a relatively small 141% in those twelve years (not enough to keep up with inflation).

Of that amount, 80.2% was disbursed for Social Security, Medicare and Federal employees' retirement benefits (combined), and...

19.8% went directly, or indirectly, to people needing unemployment assistance, family support (including AFDC), food and housing assistance, war veterans assistance, Medicaid and students' assistance (all combined).

(Source re above: *Historical Tables to the FY '95 Budget of the United States.)*

Objection: Question: Is there enough demand and liquidity in the marketplace to support the sales of assets by individuals in order to pay their Net Worth Taxes (according to the schedules in Appendix IV)?

Answer: There is more than enough liquidity if we don't wait too long to get at the problem, to wit:

To begin with, there is about $1 trillion worth of dollars trading per day in the global currency market (primarily via telecommunications between New York, London, Frankurt and Tokyo). (Source: *New York Times*, 7/24/94.)

Internally, in the U.S., the following gross assets are available:

$12.7 trillion value, total real estate including land, at market value. (Source: Federal Reserve Board, C.9 Report, p. 19, 3/9/94.)

$4.4 trillion market value of all listed stocks on the New York Stock Exchange, alone, in June 1994. (Source: New York Stock Exchange Data Base.)

> *Of that amount, more than $2 trillion is entrusted by Americans to the nation's largely unregulated 4,900 mutual funds.*
>
> (Source: Securities and Exchange Commission via New York Times, 8/9/94.)

$2.9 trillion of equities and options were sold on the U.S. Securities Exchanges in in the 12-month period from April 1993 through May 1994. (Source: *Securities and Exchange Commision Market Report, M-120,* 5/17/94.)

> Even the 96-point plunge in the Dow Jones Industrial Average (triggered by the 1/4% interest hike by the Federal Reserve Bank on 2/4/94) was hardly detectable in this trading activity. Total sales of equities in March, 1994, were $293 billion.

$3.5 trillion U.S. Federal bonds notes and bills were privately owned in the U.S. at 3/31/94. (Source: Treasury Bulletin, June, 1994.)

$1.2 trillion, Tax Exempt Bonds are outstanding in the private sector. (Source: Securities Exchange Commission, 3/10/94.)

$4.2 trillion, *M-3 Money Supply*, June, 1994 (includes currency, deposits, institutional and money market funds). (Source: Barron's Market Week, 8/8/94.)

NOTE: The above private sector assets are offset by a considerable amount of private sector debt among many accounts, as set forth in the *Balance Sheets for the U.S. Economy 1945 to 1993, C.9 Flow of Funds Report,* by the Board of Governors of the Federal Reserve System, 3/9/94 (page 7 of which is reproduced in Appendix II, hereto).

Even including the private debt offsets, the private sector net worth **balances** to $22.0 trillion.

Conclusion: The above all serves to demonstrate that there is more than enough money and liquidity in the private sector of the U.S., to support the Net Worth Tax Proposals A, B, or C, hereof, without creating undue shock to either individuals or to the economy of the U.S. as a whole.

Besides, once the Federal Debt is paid (or even partially paid), and interestt cost thereon is sharply reduced, the economy will be enormously enhanced to the benefit of all.

The Problem

Note: This is a repeated graphical plot of the data tabulated on pages 18 and 19. It shows how the national debt increased after the Nixon tax cuts in 1970 during the Vietnam War.

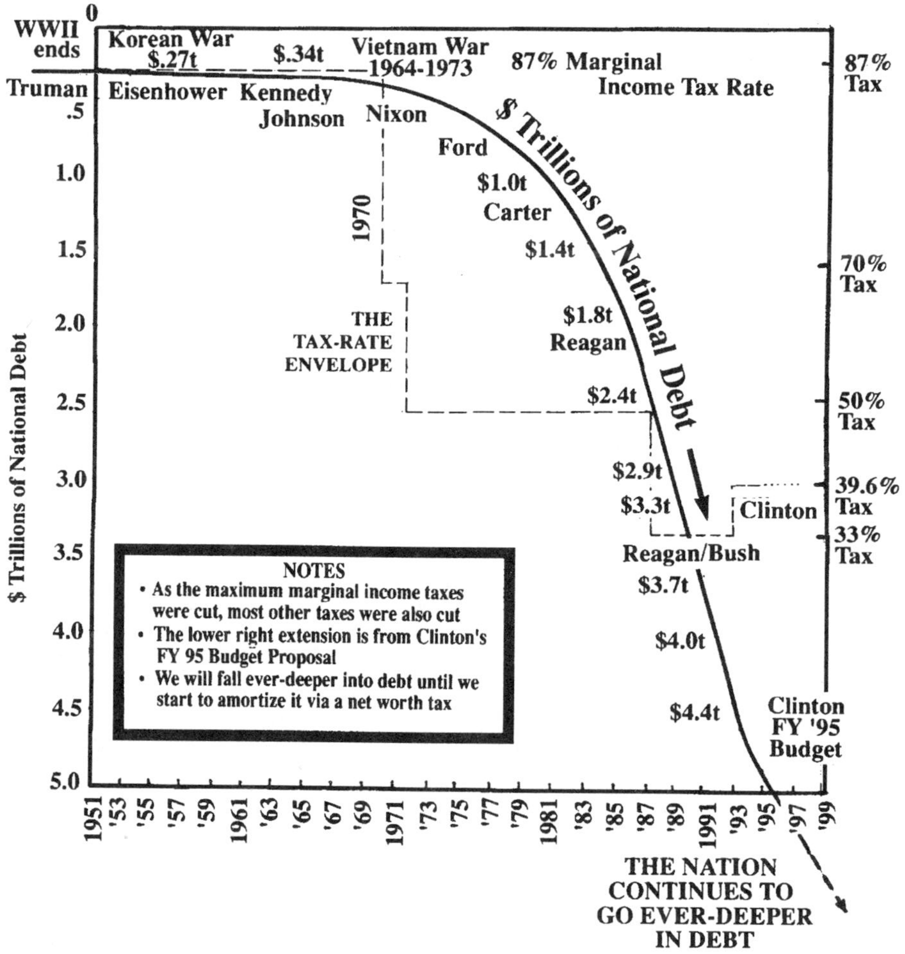

The Solution

Amortize the Debt

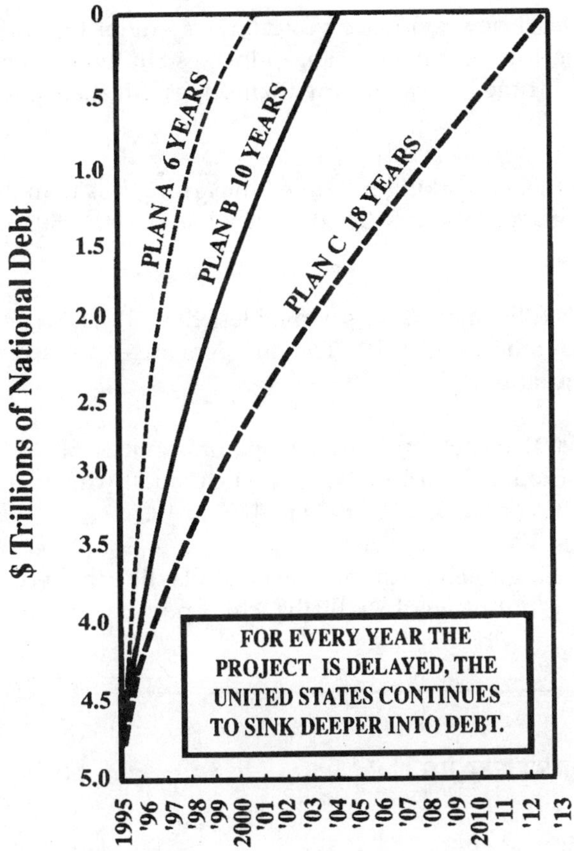

IMPORTANT HEADLINES

Please contemplate the following:

SHARP INCREASE ON THE BORDERS OF POVERTY
(New York Times 3/31/94).

"The Census Bureau provided new evidence yesterday of one of the most troubling trends in the American economy: a sharp increase in the percentage of people who work full-time but cannot, by themselves, lift their families out of poverty.

"The percentage of all Americans working full time but earning less than the poverty level for a family of four (about $13,000 a year) has risen by 50% in the past 13 years.

"In 1992, 18% of the nation's full-time workers earned less than $13,091, compared with 12% earning that amount in 1979. The numbers are expressed in 1992 dollars, adjusted for inflation.

"An annual income of $13,091 means an hourly wage of about $6.50. The percentage of full-time workers aged 18 to 24, with such small wages, has more than doubled, from 23% of workers in 1979 to 47% in 1992.

"The trend may be contributing to any number of social ills, like the record rates of welfare dependency, out-of-wedlock births, child poverty and general social disaffection..."

STUDY CONFIRMS WORST FEARS FOR U.S. CHILDREN
(New York Times 4/12/94).

The following report released today, was prepared for the Carnegie Corporation of New York by a panel of eminent doctors, educators, business executives, and politicians following a wide-ranging three-year study of young American children.

"The Carnegie study confirms some of society's worst fears. Millions of infants and toddlers are so deprived of medical care, loving supervision and intellectual stimulation that their growth into healthy and responsible adults is threatened.

"It is a picture of a United States that ranks near the bottom of the industrialized nations in providing such services as universal health care, subsidized child care and extensive leaves from work for families with children under age 3, despite recent scientific evidence that these early years are critical in the development of the human brain.

"...The quality of these young lives is deteriorating even as mounting scientific evidence indicates that children's environment, from birth to age 3, helps determine their ability to learn.

"The report asks the Federal Government to offer the States financial incentives to adopt high standards for child care and to offer training for those working in child care."

BUSH: MORE SOUL
(The Washington Times, 4/11/94;
New York Times 4/9/94)

April 8, 1994, as part of the Jimmy Carter Lecture Series at Carl Albert State College, Poteau, Oklahoma, former President George Bush sadly expressed regret for his failure to help American families more during his term in the White House, lamenting "the hollows of America's soul."

"...But if I had a chance to do one thing, it would have been to further the return to this country of an internal moral compass. We cannot continue to produce generations born into despair. We must say every choice is a moral choice, and some things are simply morally wrong."

SOCIAL SECURITY AND MEDICARE BENEFIT FUNDS WILL RUN OUT OF CASH SOON

(Newspapers nationwide, 4/12/94)

Congress requires that the Trustees for Social Security and Medicare Trust Funds (and all other trust funds for that matter) report their account balances annually to the Congress. The following information was contained in reports submitted 4/11/94:

"The Social Security Disability Trust Fund that pays benefits to disabled workers will be exhausted in 1995.

"The Medicare trust fund that pays hospital bills for the elderly will run out of money by the year 2001.

"The Trustees report shows that the financing of Medicare, the biggest Federal health program, is additionally shaky as Congress also considers programs to finance care for **39 million people** who lack health insurance.

"The part of the Social Security Trust Fund reserved for retirement programs for the elderly will be exhausted in the year 2036. By then, all people born before 1971 will be past age 65."

SMALL BUSINESS IS LARGE IN OPPOSING HEALTH PLAN

(New York Times, 4/20/94)

"The health care war these days is concentrated over the requirement that businesses must contribute to the cost of their workers health insurance. The so-called 'employer mandate' is the principal barrier to getting a health care bill out of the House Commerce Committee and the Senate Finance Committee.

"Powerful Senator Moynihan, the New York Democrat who chairs the Senate Finance Committee says that 'People are very much for the employer mandate, and very much against it.'

"The National Federation of Independent Businesses (NFIB) heads the opposition. Its Chairman, John Motley, is pleased when he says 'We're making it very difficult for them to piece things together to get this out of Committee... We're much stronger in the Senate than in the House. The Federation has mailed 600,000 pieces this year to mobilize grass roots supporters, and has 10 lobbyists on Capital Hill, and has only begun heavy barrel mailing on the Senate,' Motley says.

"Other Congressional Members (both Democrats and Republicans) say ...'this is the largest government entitlement program is history— paid for by small businesses. ...The NFIB is the same grass roots organization that has opposed working Americans' minimum wage, family and medical leave, worker safely laws... They have a strong grass roots organization that is capable of scaring people.'

"Big businesses have interests too, and are carrying a heavy share of the costs of the uninsured... They've got billions on the line (but) many of them have allowed small businesses to define the business issues in this debate.

"... Members worry about the loss of control over their employees' health plans under the Clinton proposal—being financially responsible for benefit packages determined by Washington."

Author's Comments and recommendations:

1) Install a Net Worth tax to reduce the Federal debt.

2) The U.S. Government pay for **all** the services and insurances, and

3) Drop the whole idea of passing these extra cost-burdens on to business es, which are just going to "take it out" on their working employees.

4) If we can all agree to pay the debt, we can free-up enough cash to do almost anything we want to do. And that needs to be done.

THE ONLY ANSWER? AGREE TO PAY THE DEBT! AND BREAK THE DEADLOCKS AND GRIDBLOCKS IN CONGRESS.

PART III

POLITICAL ACTION NEEDED IN 1994

TO ALL CANDIDATES FOR CONGRESS IN 1994:

I mailed copies of this book to all members of Congress, the President,Vice President all Cabinet Members and all key staff officers the day it came off the presses.

You must understand that, under this plan, 80% of all voters (that is, all those households who have less than $150,000 net worth) would not be required to pay any Net Worth Tax at all...

And when those voters, and many others, see the advantages of having an economically more-level playing field than otherwise provided for their worrisome past, present and future...

> *Then, you had better understand and believe that they will not vote for you unless and until you speak and write in favor of this debt reduction plan during your 1994 campaigns.*

You can tell the voters that this debt-elimination proposal is what will make their universal health insurance coverage possible. You can tell them that this way has a far better chance than any other to provide greater employment at higher wages...and better living conditions generally than does any more "conservative" plan.

Then, and only then, I believe, will you have a chance to win your elections. Because the majority of voters are "fed up" with the lack of direction, and the endless bickering and waste of time and money by Congress.

And most people are exceedingly frightened by the ever-increasing debt and the disaster it could mean for themselves and this country.

AND TO ALL VOTERS IN 1994:

I, personally, have already started to push Congress.

I have written to my district Representatives in the House and Senate (and to prospective-1994 candidates) *that I will not support or vote for them* unless they publicly commit, in advance, to support a new tax law, in 1995, to start to reduce the Federal debt via a Net Worth Tax.

I urge all voters to do the same in regard to their own Congressional-representatives and candidates...no matter to which party they belong...because, to succeed, this must be a non-partisan veter-driven political effort.

> The threat of a majority of votes, so cast, is the only language politicians will understand.

See Appendix VI for the name, address and telephone number of your representative and Senators.

And to Senators Dole, Gramm, Kassebaum and Packwood, and Representatives Gingrich, Armey...and all of you others who voted against the Clinton tax bill August 5 and 6, 1993... I suggest that you drop your unreasoning stands against more taxes, and, instead, get behind this program to pay the debt and prevent national bankruptcy. As a result, Congress can then balance the budget, and not until then.

Voters should note that Dan Quayle (who wants to be President) did not mention the National Debt his in recent book, *Standing Firm*.

Neither did Oliver North as he announced for the Virginia Senate seat.

Both Quayle and North are multimillionaires and stand for lower taxes. They have proposed no way to balance the budget, except to take away "entitlements" from those citizens who need them most.

ACKNOWLEDGMENTS ARE OWING TO THE FOLLOWING:

INFORM Research Group, Minneapolis Public Library, Minneapolis, Minnesota. Particularly, Roger Hurd, INFORM Librarian, and Wendy Adamson, Librarian.

Ambra Nava McCain, Computer Operator, helped me get started on text.

It would have been categorically impossible for me to have organized and prepared this book without the very special talents of Catherine Keenan, who by her computer skills organized and prepared the Debt Amortization and Net Worth Tax Tables, Appendix IV, and summaries thereof, pages 51–53 plus text organization, preparation and layout.

Vanessa Davisson was the graphic design, pre-production and pre-publishing specialist.

My particular thanks to the competent staff at Carlton Press Corp., New York, N.Y. for their enthusiastic and dynamic work as Publishers. They literally had this book published and in the marketplace six weeks after we signed a contract.

Participants included my family and many friends, and acquaintances old and new. And mentors from many years back. You all know who you are. Thanks to you all.

In particular, my wonderful wife of 45 years, Laura H. Miles, lawyer, artist and mother of three, was insightful, encouraging, helpful and exceedingly patient throughout.

POSTSCRIPT

I first started thinking about the debt subject two years ago, when, like Paul Revere, Ross Perot first raised the $4 trillion debt-alarm. But Perot wrote and talked only about reducing the annual deficit to the end of the century. He repeated "no more taxes." He said nothing about a program to reduce or amortize the ever-growing Federal debt.

I seriously started writing this book in May 1993, and I've been at it day and night ever since, as my good wife, Laura, can attest.

How many drafts and redrafts? I've lost count.

I "tested" each draft against, first a few, then dozens and even hundreds of friends and acquaintances at all levels of wealth and non-wealth...Republicans, Democrats and Independents. I included shop owners, clerks, lawyers, doctors, professors, tax accountants, laborers, people in their working years, retired folks, syndicated columnists, news and book publishers, and top executives (both within and outside of Government).

Also, dozens of telephone operators and secretaries in most Departments in Washington to whom I told of the $5 trillion dollar debt book I was writing (and who always expressed their concerns about the debt)... often with a "Mr. Miles? Oh yes, I remember you and your $5 trillion book. How may I help you today?"

Many people passed drafts on to others. All said they hadn't seen anything like it before, and that, having picked it up, they couldn't stop reading until they completed it. Most read it 2 or 3 times.

A number wrote very sharp criticisms which I tried to answer, and which forced me to rethink and reresearch the facts and data and conclusions. And rewrite. And resubmit.

Most were then satisfied with the results, saying, "Yes, I guess you're right. Keep at it!" One nationally syndicated weekly columnist wrote: "Best of luck...you'll <u>never, never</u> be sorry you took on this project."

The process was often a headache. Never a bore. I concentrated on the facts, nothing but the facts...many of which, unfortunately, were not widely known or understood.

As I finish writing this book in September, 1994, it greatly concerns me that so little is known by so many people regarding the size and nature of our Federal debt, and the damage it is doing to our national well-being... particularly to the millions of people whose circumstances are the least fortunate.

The debt is like a gigantic cancerous tumor. It is growing unabatedly, at a fantastic rate. In effect, we are sick inside, but we don't yet perceive it.

Like many progressive illnesses, this thing has already reached the stage where it is affecting not only our physical beings, but also our minds. Feelings of insecurity, anxiety, foreboding and malaise have become part of the national syndrome.

The debt-danger must be of great concern to President Clinton.

> But *how* does he bring up a subject as scary as this to the American people?
>
> And *who* among his staff (or in the Congress) has come up with a solution to the problem?

Those questions remain unanswered for him, as they do for all of us.

All the facts are here available. The purpose of this book has been to integrate them and bring them forward for us all to see and understand.

Time is of the essence.

James G. Miles, September, 1994.

1600 Pennsylvania Ave., N.W.
Washington, D.C. 20500

Hillary Rodham Clinton

Thank you for sharing your ideas and suggestions. Bill and I welcome your thoughts. They will be carefully considered as Bill begins to implement his agenda for change in America.

Best wishes, Hillary

WASHINGTON, DC 203
PM
12 MAR
1993

Mr. James G. Miles
Box 1346
Rio Verde, Arizona 85263-1346

Autobiography: James G. Miles, Author,

I am happily "retired" after over fifty years in business...all of them productive. I am fortunate to have had good foresight and have always been at the cutting edge.

With two degrees in electronic engineering from the University of Nebraska, I was one of the pioneers in the computer industry starting in 1946. Working on a then secret project of the U.S. Navy Computing Machine Laboratory (USNCML), St. Paul, Minnesota, I was the inventor of the selectively-alterable magnetic disc memory (1947–1948)... a working prototype of the magnetic storage disks widely used in today's computers.

Picking up a degree in business law from William Mitchell College of Law, St. Paul, Minnesota in 1949, I switched over to computer sales and sold the first airline reservation system to Captain Eddie Rickenbacker, President of Eastern Air Lines in 1953.

I was one of the founders of Control Data Corporation in 1957...initially V.P. for U.S. Government sales. Then, from 1960, I was marketing V.P. for "TRTW" (the rest of the world). As Control Data's primary door-opener, we successfully sold CDC's advanced scientific computers to leaders in 25 countries.

As an unpaid volunteer, I was on many U.S. Government, State and local advisory panels, including the U.S. Export Expansion Council in the 1960's and early 70's.

In 1974, I resigned from CDC to run for Governor of Minnesota as an Independent candidate. My wife, Laura H. Miles, was Lieutenant Governor running mate. We didn't win, but came in a strong third out of a field of eight. Most importantly, we left a permanent mark on Minnesota politics and on the State's Administrative and Court systems.

After 1974, I became an independent venture capitalist and marketer, helped start 15 new ventures in Minnesota.

As a volunteer from 1967 to 1972, I was Board Chairman and helped found the then-new and now outstanding Minneapolis Children's Hospital.

In virtually all of those earlier enterprises, I successfully employed the financial-analyses and program techniques of this book.

While writing this book, I have been in touch with the Clinton Administration and key Congressional members of both parties to get *debt-reduction* as a priority-item on the national agenda in 1994.

Laura H. Miles, my helpful and supportive wife of 45 years, and I have three professionally-active sons and daughters (and 6 grands), all living in the Minneapolis area. Our son Steven H. Miles, M.D., has been on the Clinton Health Care Task Force and continues to work with Congressional Committees concerned with health care programming and financing.

APPENDICES

APPENDIX I
FY '95 BUDGET PROPOSAL

APPENDIX II
NET WORTH OF U.S. PRIVATE SECTOR

APPENDIX III
FAMILY NET WORTH TABLES

APPENDIX IV
DEBT AMORTIZATION AND TAX PLANS

APPENDIX V
ITEMS TO BE DECLARED

APPENDIX VI
CONGRESSIONAL DIRECTORY

Appendix I:
Summaries: Clinton FY '95 Budget Proposal

Reproduction

THE FEDERAL GOVERNMENT DOLLAR
FISCAL YEAR 1995 ESTIMATES

WHERE IT COMES FROM...

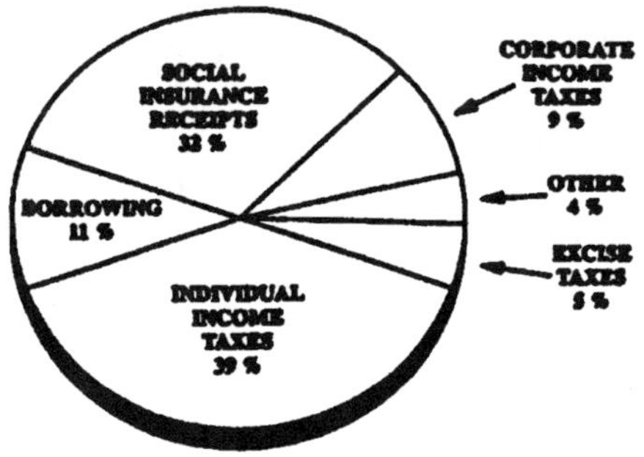

WHERE IT GOES...

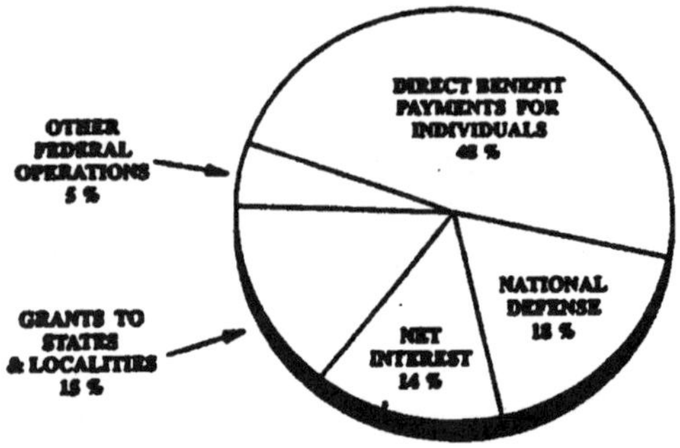

Appendix I:
Summaries: Clinton FY '95 Budget Proposal

INTRODUCTION:
AN OVERVIEW OF THE 1995 BUDGET

Table I–1. OUTLAYS, RECEIPTS AND DEFICIT SUMMARY
(Dollar amounts in billions)

	1993	1994	1995	1996	1997	1998	1999
Outlays:							
Discretionary	542.5	550.1	542.4	543.9	564.3	548.1	554.4
Mandatory:							
Deposit insurance	−28.0	−8.3	−11.1	−11.3	−6.1	−4.9	−3.3
Other mandatory	694.9	738.7	774.0	826.1	867.5	949.9	1,023.8
Subtotal, mandatory	666.9	730.4	762.9	814.9	861.4	945.0	1,020.5
Net interest	198.8	203.4	213.1	224.8	234.6	245.0	255.2
Total outlays	1,408.2	1,484.0	1,518.3	1,583.5	1,660.3	1,738.2	1,830.2
Receipts	1,153.5	1,249.2	1,342.2	1,410.4	1,479.5	1,550.8	1,629.0
Deficit	254.7	234.8	176.1	173.1	180.8	187.4	201.2
Totals as a percent of GDP:							
Outlays	22.4%	22.3%	21.6%	21.3%	21.2%	21.0%	20.9%
Receipts	18.3%	18.8%	19.1%	19.0%	18.9%	18.7%	18.6%
Deficit	4.0%	3.5%	2.5%	2.3%	2.3%	2.3%	2.3%
Memorandum—Totals with health reform:							
Deficit	254.7	234.8	165.1	169.6	186.4	190.5	181.1
Deficit as a percent of GDP	4.0%	3.5%	2.4%	2.3%	2.4%	2.3%	2.1%

Table I–2. ECONOMIC ASSUMPTIONS[1]
(Calendar years)

	1992 Actual	Projections 1993	1994	1995	1996	1997	1998	1999
Gross Domestic Product (GDP):								
Percent change, fourth quarter over fourth quarter:								
Current dollars	6.7	5.0	5.8	5.6	5.7	5.7	5.7	5.6
Constant (1987) dollars	3.9	2.3	3.0	2.7	2.7	2.6	2.6	2.5
Implicit price deflator (1987 = 100)	2.8	2.6	2.7	2.8	2.9	3.0	3.0	3.0
Consumer Price Index (all urban):[2]								
Percent change, fourth quarter over fourth quarter	3.1	2.8	3.0	3.2	3.3	3.4	3.4	3.4
Unemployment rate, civilian, percent:[3]								
Fourth quarter level	7.3	6.7	6.4	6.0	5.8	5.6	5.5	5.5
Interest rates, percent:								
91-day Treasury bills[4]	3.5	3.0	3.4	3.8	4.1	4.4	4.4	4.4
10-year Treasury notes	7.0	5.9	5.8	5.8	5.8	5.8	5.8	5.8

[1] Based on information available as of December 1993.
[2] CPI for all urban consumers.
[3] Pre-1994 basis. A February 1994 change in survey methodology is expected to add about 0.5 percentage points to the measured unemployment rate.
[4] Average rate (bank discount basis) on new issues within period.

Appendix II: Net Worth of the Private Sector of the U.S.

Source: Federal Reserve Board Balance Sheets of the U.S. Economy 1945-1993 , C.9 Flow of Funds, March 9, 1994 Reproduction

B.11 Domestic Wealth with Tangible Assets at Current Cost Year-End Outstandings

	1990	1991	1992	1993	Data are in billions of dollars.	
1	18255.1	18405.2	18363.2	18765.0	Domestic wealth (1)	1
2	18233.1	18382.9	18343.6	18744.9	Total tangible assets (2)	2
3	13274.0	13637.6	14056.0	14514.8	Reproducible assets (3)	3
4	4795.8	4972.1	5190.6	5499.2	Residential structures	4
5	5326.7	5440.2	5534.3	5544.2	Nonres. plant & equip.	5
6	1110.4	1083.4	1099.0	1133.4	Inventories	6
7	2047.1	2141.9	2232.1	2338.0	Consumer durables	7
8	4959.1	4745.3	4287.6	4230.0	Land at market value	8
9	22.0	22.3	19.6	20.1	+ U.S. monetary gold & SDRs	9
10	18255.1	18405.2	18363.2	18765.0	Domestic net worth, by sector (4)(5)	10
11	20808.2	21200.1	21386.6	21966.2	Private sector net worth, consolidated (6)	11
12	11604.2	12123.9	12553.4	13066.9	Household net assets	12
13	18933.1	20731.8	21766.4	22742.3	Sector net worth	13
14	2440.6	2344.6	2274.5	2221.2	-Equity in noncorp. bus.	14
15	1738.7	2482.8	2884.3	3009.4	-Corp. equities held (7)(8)	15
16	3149.8	3780.4	4054.3	4444.8	-Pension fund reserves	16
17	6577.9	6284.2	5977.2	5989.3	Nonfinan. business net worth	17
18	1713.5	1631.4	1546.9	1498.0	Nonfarm noncorp. business	18
19	776.1	764.7	781.6	787.4	Farm business	19
20	4088.5	3888.1	3648.7	3703.8	Nonfinancial corps.	20
21	2626.1	2792.0	2856.1	2910.0	Pvt. finan. inst. net assets	21
22	1059.6	1126.3	1158.0	1256.0	Sector net worth	22
23	3149.6	3780.4	4054.3	4444.8	+Pension fund reserves	23
24	1568.8	2114.8	2356.2	2798.7	-Corp. equities held (7)(8)	24
25	-2507.9	-2782.0	-3182.1	-3525.3	Public sector net assets	25
26	-136.6	-173.2	-227.4	-288.7	State and local governments	26
27	-2406.0	-2646.5	-2998.2	-3285.7	U.S. government	27
28	33.1	36.0	41.8	47.3	Govt.-spons. enterprises	28
29	1.6	1.7	1.7	1.8	Monetary authority	29
					Less:	
30	-306.4	-357.0	-475.9	-652.5	Net U.S. financial claims on foreigners (9)	30
31	1216.3	1230.2	1263.1	1329.9	Fgn.assets of U.S. residents	31
32	1522.7	1587.2	1739.0	1982.4	-Total U.S. assets held by foreigners, excluding equities	32
33	-351.6	-369.9	-317.3	-328.5	Unallocated finan.assets (10)	33

(1) Located within U.S. geographical boundaries.
(2) Excludes tangible assets of federal, state, and local governments; excludes land holdings of Federal Reserve Banks and government-sponsored enterprises; excludes investments in intangible assets such as patents.
(3) At current cost.
(4) National net worth equals domestic net worth plus U.S. net claims on foreigners (lines 10 + 30).
(5) Equals net consolidated tangible and financial assets of public and private sectors, less net U.S. financial claims on foreigners, plus unallocated financial assets (lines 11 + 25 - 30 + 33).
(6) Lines 12 + 17 + 21.
(7) Includes holdings of foreign equities.
(8) Excludes mutual fund shares.
(9) Excludes U.S. holdings of foreign equities and foreign holdings of U.S. equities.
(10) Statistical discrepancy. Equals the sum of differences between liabilities for and holdings of individual financial instruments arises from timing and reporting differences

Appendix III: Family Net Worth Tables
Distribution of Wealth in the U.S.
Source: House of Representatives 1993 *Green Book,* p. 1558
Reproduction

TABLE 6.—1983 AND 1989 MEAN AND MEDIAN NET WORTH, BY FAMILY CHARACTERISTIC

[In 1989 dollars]

Family characteristic	1983			1989		
	Percent of families	Net worth		Percent of families	Net worth	
		Mean	Median		Mean	Median
All families	100	$149,100	$42,700	100	$183,700	$47,200
Family income (1989 dollars):						
Less than 10,000	19	30,000	3,800	20	30,100	2,300
10,000–19,999	23	53,000	19,300	20	63,100	27,100
20,000–29,999	19	69,500	36,900	17	89,600	37,000
30,000–49,999	23	117,600	67,700	23	150,200	69,200
50,000 and more	17	550,500	176,100	20	586,700	185,600
Age of family head (years):						
Under 35	31	40,900	8,500	26	46,900	6,800
35–44	19	110,500	49,800	23	148,300	52,800
45–54	15	215,900	69,400	14	286,400	86,700
55–64	15	242,200	84,400	15	292,500	91,300
65–74	12	272,600	76,300	13	278,300	77,600
75 and over	7	166,800	49,800	9	194,500	66,100
Education of family head:						
0–8 grades	15	59,000	24,400	13	77,200	27,300
9–11 grades	13	68,200	23,000	11	80,500	27,300
High school diploma	31	103,600	41,800	32	109,600	37,100
Some college	18	172,200	42,300	15	171,900	46,900
College degree	23	297,800	89,500	29	364,600	104,700
Race of family head:						
White	82	173,000	54,300	87	203,800	58,500
Nonwhite and Hispanic	18	37,600	6,900	13	45,900	4,000
Life-cycle stage of family head:						
Under 55 years:						
Unmarried, no children	11	48,900	6,000	11	47,500	8,400
Married, no children	6	80,100	20,100	5	147,900	27,300
Unmarried, children	13	57,800	10,800	13	54,200	5,700
Married, children	35	140,600	51,300	34	196,900	62,000
55 years and over:						
In labor force	14	363,100	108,000	12	438,300	104,500
Out of labor force:						
Retired	18	153,600	63,900	18	211,600	94,100
Other	3	123,800	51,000	7	87,600	33,200
Housing status:						
Own	63	219,600	80,400	65	266,900	97,300
Rent or other	37	26,800	3,000	35	31,208	2,200

Source: Adapted from: Arthur B. Kennickell and Janice Shack-Marquez, "Changes in Family Finances from 1983 to 1989: Evidence from the Survey of Consumer Finances," Federal Reserve Bulletin, January 1992.

Distribution of Wealth in the U.S.

Source: Federal Resource Bulletin, 1/92

Reproduction

No. 732. Family Net Worth—Mean and Median of Net Worth, by Selected Characteristics: 1983 and 1989

[Mean and median value in thousands of constant 1989 dollars. Constant dollar figures are based on consumer price index data published by U.S. Bureau of Labor Statistics: see table 738, section 15. See headnote, table 733]

CHARACTERISTIC	1983			1989		
	Percent of families	Net worth		Percent of families	Net worth	
		Mean	Median		Mean	Median
All families	100	149.1	42.7	100	183.7	47.2
White	82	173.0	54.3	87	203.8	58.5
Nonwhite and Hispanic	18	37.6	6.9	13	45.9	4.0
Under 35 years old	31	40.9	8.5	26	46.9	6.8
35 to 44 years old	19	110.5	49.8	23	148.3	52.8
45 to 54 years old	15	215.9	69.4	14	286.4	86.7
55 to 64 years old	15	242.2	84.4	15	292.5	91.3
65 to 74 years old	12	272.6	76.3	13	278.3	77.6
75 years old and over	7	166.8	49.8	9	194.5	66.1
Under 55 years old:						
Unmarried, no children	11	48.9	6.0	11	47.5	8.4
Married, no children	6	80.1	20.1	5	147.9	27.3
Unmarried, children	13	57.8	10.8	13	54.2	5.7
Married, children	35	140.6	51.3	34	196.9	62.0
55 years and over:						
In labor force	14	363.1	108.0	12	438.3	104.5
Retired	18	153.6	63.9	18	211.6	94.1
Managerial and professional specialities	24	328.5	95.8	25	382.0	104.5
Technical, sales, and administrative support	12	105.1	39.1	12	139.7	32.6
Service occupations	7	33.6	12.1	7	46.1	8.4
Precision production, craft, and repair	12	70.4	40.0	12	91.5	46.0
Operators, fabricators, and laborers	12	49.3	28.6	9	67.3	18.8
Farming, forestry, and fishing	2	343.9	185.0	2	322.3	107.3
Not working	31	110.7	30.0	33	138.9	44.0
Income (1989 dollars):						
Less than $10,000	19	30.0	3.8	20	30.1	2.3
$10,000 to $19,999	23	53.0	19.3	20	63.1	27.1
$20,000 to $29,999	19	69.5	36.9	17	69.6	37.0
$30,000 to $49,999	23	117.6	67.7	23	150.2	69.2
$50,000 and over	17	550.5	176.1	20	586.7	185.6

Source: Board of Governors of the Federal Reserve System, *Federal Reserve Bulletin*, January 1992.

APPENDIX IV

AMORTIZATION AND TAX PLANS

PLAN A, 6 YEARS

PLAN B, 10 YEARS

PLAN C, 18 YEARS

Amortization Plan A, year 1

NET WORTH TAX TABLE for 1994 (payable by 4/15/95)

Plan A - Based on 100% maximum proposed amortization rate

Note: These data are projected from the same sources as shown on Distribution of Wealth Graph, p36, and Appendix II, and do not indicate household yearly increases or decreases except for Net Worth Taxes paid. Tables for subsequent years follow on sequential pages. All tables are summarized page 51-53.

Bracket	Household Net Worth dollars	Number of Households	end 1994 per Household av Net Worth dollars	end 1994 Bracket Group Net Worth dollars	NW Tax yearly percent	Pay by 4/15/95 Net Worth Tax Av Household dollars	Pay by 4/15/95 Bracket Group Net Worth Tax dollars	After 4/15/95 per Household av Net Worth dollars
0	under 150K	80,000,000	100,000	8,000,000,000,000	0.0%	0	0	100,000
1	150-200K	10,000,000	175,000	1,750,000,000,000	1.0%	1,750	17,500,000,000	173,250
2	200-600K	5,000,000	400,000	2,000,000,000,000	2.0%	8,000	40,000,000,000	392,000
3	600-800K	3,000,000	700,000	2,100,000,000,000	3.0%	21,000	63,000,000,000	679,000
4	800K-1.5M	1,000,000	1,200,000	1,200,000,000,000	4.0%	48,000	48,000,000,000	1,152,000
5	1.5-4M	500,000	3,600,000	1,800,000,000,000	5.0%	180,000	90,000,000,000	3,420,000
6	4-5M	300,000	3,528,000	1,058,400,000,000	6.0%	211,680	63,504,000,000	3,316,320
7	5-6.5M	140,000	5,733,000	802,620,000,000	8.0%	458,640	64,209,600,000	5,274,360
8	6.5-15M	25,000	12,348,000	308,700,000,000	10.0%	1,234,800	30,870,000,000	11,113,200
9	15-35M	12,000	30,870,000	370,440,000,000	12.0%	3,704,400	44,452,800,000	27,165,600
10	35-65M	10,000	57,330,000	573,300,000,000	16.0%	9,172,800	91,728,000,000	48,157,200
11	65-135M	7,000	114,660,000	802,620,000,000	20.0%	22,932,000	160,524,000,000	91,728,000
12	135-185M	3,000	176,400,000	529,200,000,000	30.0%	52,920,000	158,760,000,000	123,480,000
13	185-260M	1,000	255,780,000	255,780,000,000	32.0%	81,849,600	81,849,600,000	173,930,400
14	260-400M	900	352,800,000	317,520,000,000	35.0%	123,480,000	111,132,000,000	229,320,000
15	400-500M	400	467,460,000	186,984,000,000	38.0%	177,634,800	71,053,920,000	289,825,200
16	500-900M	320	705,600,000	225,792,000,000	40.0%	282,240,000	90,316,800,000	423,360,000
17	900-1.2B	180	1,146,600,000	206,388,000,000	43.0%	493,038,000	88,746,840,000	653,562,000
18	1.2B-3.0B	125	2,469,600,000	308,700,000,000	45.0%	1,111,320,000	138,915,000,000	1,358,280,000
19	3.0-7B	60	6,174,000,000	370,440,000,000	48.0%	2,963,520,000	177,811,200,000	3,210,480,000
20	7 Bil or more	15	12,348,000,000	185,220,000,000	50.0%	6,174,000,000	92,610,000,000	6,174,000,000
Total		100,000,000		23,352,104,000,000			1,724,983,760,000	
							paid into U.S. Treasury	

Amortization Plan A, year 2

NET WORTH TAX TABLE for 1995 (payable by 4/15/96)

Plan A - Based on 100% maximum proposed amortization rate

Note: These data are projected from the same sources as shown on Distribution of Wealth Graph, p36, and Appendix II, and do not indicate household yearly increases or decreases except for Net Worth Taxes paid. Tables for subsequent years follow on sequential pages. All tables are summarized page 51-53.

Bracket	Household Net Worth dollars	Number of Households	end 1995 per Household av Net Worth dollars	end 1995 Bracket Group Net Worth dollars	NW Tax yearly percent	Pay by 4/15/96 Net Worth Tax Av Household dollars	Pay by 4/15/96 Bracket Group Net Worth Tax dollars	After 4/15/96 per Household av Net Worth dollars
0	under 150K	80,000,000	100,000	8,000,000,000,000	0.0%	0	0	100,000
1	150-200K	10,000,000	173,250	1,732,500,000,000	1.0%	1,733	17,325,000,000	171,518
2	200-600K	5,000,000	392,000	1,960,000,000,000	2.0%	7,840	39,200,000,000	384,160
3	600-800K	3,000,000	679,000	2,037,000,000,000	3.0%	20,370	61,110,000,000	658,630
4	800K-1.5M	1,000,000	1,152,000	1,152,000,000,000	4.0%	46,080	46,080,000,000	1,105,920
5	1.5-4M	800,000	3,368,160	2,694,528,000,000	5.0%	168,408	134,726,400,000	3,199,752
6	4-5M	0	0	0	6.0%	0	0	0
7	5-6.5M	140,000	5,274,360	738,410,400,000	8.0%	421,949	59,072,832,000	4,852,411
8	6.5-15M	25,000	11,113,200	277,830,000,000	10.0%	1,111,320	27,783,000,000	10,001,880
9	15-35M	12,000	27,165,600	325,987,200,000	12.0%	3,259,872	39,118,464,000	23,905,728
10	35-65M	10,000	48,157,200	481,572,000,000	16.0%	7,705,152	77,051,520,000	40,452,048
11	65-135M	7,000	91,728,000	642,096,000,000	20.0%	18,345,600	128,419,200,000	73,382,400
12	135-185M	3,000	123,480,000	370,440,000,000	30.0%	37,044,000	111,132,000,000	86,436,000
13	185-260M	1,000	173,930,400	173,930,400,000	32.0%	55,657,728	55,657,728,000	118,272,672
14	260-400M	1,300	259,572,600	337,444,380,000	35.0%	90,850,410	118,105,533,000	168,722,190
15	400-500M	0	0	0	38.0%	0	0	0
16	500-900M	500	538,461,000	269,230,500,000	40.0%	215,384,400	107,692,200,000	323,076,600
17	900-1.2B	0	0	0	43.0%	0	0	0
18	1.2B-3.0B	125	1,358,280,000	169,785,000,000	45.0%	611,226,000	76,403,250,000	747,054,000
19	3.0-7B	60	3,210,480,000	192,628,800,000	48.0%	1,541,030,400	92,461,824,000	1,669,449,600
20	7 Bil or more	15	6,174,000,000	92,610,000,000	50.0%	3,087,000,000	46,305,000,000	3,087,000,000
Total		100,000,000		21,647,992,680,000			1,237,643,951,000	
							paid into U.S. Treasury	

Amortization Plan A, year 3

NET WORTH TAX TABLE for 1996 (payable by 4/15/97)

Plan A - Based on 100% maximum proposed amortization rate

Note: These data are projected from the same sources as shown on Distribution of Wealth Graph, p36, and Appendix II, and do not indicate household yearly increases or decreases except for Net Worth Taxes paid. Tables for subsequent years follow on sequential pages. All tables are summarized page 51-53.

Bracket	Household Net Worth dollars	Number of Households	end 1996 per Household av Net Worth dollars	end 1996 Bracket Group Net Worth dollars	NW Tax yearly percent	Pay by 4/15/97 Net Worth Tax Av Household dollars	Pay by 4/15/97 Bracket Group Net Worth Tax dollars	After 4/15/97 per Household av Net Worth dollars
0	under 150K	80,000,000	100,000	8,000,000,000,000	0.0%	0	0	100,000
1	150-200K	10,000,000	171,518	1,715,175,000,000	1.0%	1,715	17,151,750,000	169,802
2	200-600K	5,000,000	384,160	1,920,800,000,000	2.0%	7,683	38,416,000,000	376,477
3	600-800K	3,000,000	658,630	1,975,890,000,000	3.0%	19,759	59,276,700,000	638,871
4	800K-1.5M	1,000,000	1,105,920	1,105,920,000,000	4.0%	44,237	44,236,800,000	1,061,683
5	1.5-4M	800,000	3,199,752	2,559,801,600,000	5.0%	159,988	127,990,080,000	3,039,764
6	4-5M	0	0	0	6.0%	0	0	0
7	5-6.5M	140,000	4,852,411	679,337,568,000	8.0%	388,193	54,347,005,440	4,464,218
8	6.5-15M	25,000	10,001,880	250,047,000,000	10.0%	1,000,188	25,004,700,000	9,001,692
9	15-35M	12,000	23,905,728	286,868,736,000	12.0%	2,868,687	34,424,248,320	21,037,041
10	35-65M	10,000	40,452,048	404,520,480,000	16.0%	6,472,328	64,723,276,800	33,979,720
11	65-135M	10,000	79,909,200	799,092,000,000	20.0%	15,981,840	159,818,400,000	63,927,360
12	135-185M	1,000	118,272,672	118,272,672,000	30.0%	35,481,802	35,481,801,600	82,790,870
13	185-260M	1,300	168,722,190	219,338,847,000	32.0%	53,991,101	70,188,431,040	114,731,089
14	260-400M	0	0	0	35.0%	0	0	0
15	400-500M	500	323,076,600	161,538,300,000	38.0%	122,769,108	61,384,554,000	200,307,492
16	500-900M	0	0	0	40.0%	0	0	0
17	900-1.2B	125	747,054,000	93,381,750,000	43.0%	321,233,220	40,154,152,500	425,820,780
18	1.2B-3.0B	60	1,669,449,600	100,166,976,000	45.0%	751,252,320	45,075,139,200	918,197,280
19	3.0-7B	15	3,087,000,000	46,305,000,000	48.0%	1,481,760,000	22,226,400,000	1,605,240,000
20	7 Bil or more	0	0	0	50.0%	0	0	0
Total		100,000,000		20,436,455,929,000			899,899,438,900	
							paid into U.S. Treasury	

Amortization Plan A, year 4

NET WORTH TAX TABLE for 1997 (payable by 4/15/98)

Plan A - Based on 100% maximum proposed amortization rate

Note: These data are projected from the same sources as shown on Distribution of Wealth Graph, p36, and Appendix II, and do not indicate household yearly increases or decreases except for Net Worth Taxes paid. Tables for subsequent years follow on sequential pages. All tables are summarized page 51-53.

Bracket	Household Net Worth dollars	Number of Households	end 1997 per Household av Net Worth dollars	end 1997 Bracket Group Net Worth dollars	NW Tax yearly percent	Pay by 4/15/98 Net Worth Tax Av Household dollars	Pay by 4/15/98 Bracket Group Net Worth Tax dollars	After 4/15/98 per Household av Net Worth dollars
0	under 150K	80,000,000	100,000	8,000,000,000,000	0.0%	0	0	100,000
1	150-200K	10,000,000	169,802	1,698,023,250,000	1.0%	1,698	16,980,232,500	168,104
2	200-600K	5,000,000	376,477	1,882,384,000,000	2.0%	7,530	37,647,680,000	368,947
3	600-800K	3,000,000	638,871	1,916,613,300,000	3.0%	19,166	57,498,399,000	619,705
4	800K-1.5M	1,000,000	1,061,683	1,061,683,200,000	4.0%	42,467	42,467,328,000	1,019,216
5	1.5-4M	800,000	3,039,764	2,431,811,520,000	5.0%	151,988	121,590,576,000	2,887,776
6	4-5M	140,000	4,464,218	624,990,562,560	6.0%	267,853	37,499,433,754	4,196,365
7	5-6.5M	0	0	0	8.0%	0	0	0
8	6.5-15M	25,000	9,001,692	225,042,300,000	10.0%	900,169	22,504,230,000	8,101,523
9	15-35M	12,000	21,037,041	252,444,487,680	12.0%	2,524,445	30,293,338,522	18,512,596
10	35-65M	10,000	33,979,720	339,797,203,200	16.0%	5,436,755	54,367,552,512	28,542,965
11	65-135M	11,000	73,359,115	806,950,267,200	20.0%	14,671,823	161,390,053,440	58,687,292
12	135-185M	1,300	114,731,089	149,150,415,960	30.0%	34,419,327	44,745,124,788	80,311,762
13	185-260M	0	0	0	32.0%	0	0	0
14	260-400M	500	200,307,492	100,153,746,000	35.0%	70,107,622	35,053,811,100	130,199,870
15	400-500M	0	0	0	38.0%	0	0	0
16	500-900M	125	425,820,780	53,227,597,500	40.0%	170,328,312	21,291,039,000	255,492,468
17	900-1.2B	0	0	0	43.0%	0	0	0
18	1.2B-3.0B	60	918,197,280	55,091,836,800	45.0%	413,188,776	24,791,326,560	505,008,504
19	3.0-7B	15	1,605,240,000	24,078,600,000	48.0%	770,515,200	11,557,728,000	834,724,800
20	7 Bil or more	0	0	0	50.0%	0	0	0
Total		100,000,000		19,621,442,286,900			719,677,853,175	
							paid into U.S. Treasury	

Amortization Plan A, year 5

NET WORTH TAX TABLE for 1998 (payable by 4/15/99)

Plan A - Based on 100% maximum proposed amortization rate

Note: These data are projected from the same sources as shown on Distribution of Wealth Graph, p36, and Appendix II, and do not indicate household yearly increases or decreases except for Net Worth Taxes paid.
Tables for subsequent years follow on sequential pages. All tables are summarized page 51-53.

Bracket	Household Net Worth dollars	Number of Households	end 1998 per Household av Net Worth dollars	end 1998 Bracket Group Net Worth dollars	NW Tax yearly percent	Pay by 4/15/99 Net Worth Tax Av Household dollars	Pay by 4/15/99 Bracket Group Net Worth Tax dollars	After 4/15/99 per Household av Net Worth dollars
0	under 150K	80,000,000	100,000	8,000,000,000,000	0.0%	0	0	100,000
1	150-200K	10,000,000	168,104	1,681,043,017,500	1.0%	1,681	16,810,430,175	166,423
2	200-600K	5,000,000	368,947	1,844,736,320,000	2.0%	7,379	36,894,726,400	361,568
3	600-800K	3,000,000	619,705	1,859,114,901,000	3.0%	18,591	55,773,447,030	601,114
4	800K-1.5M	1,000,000	1,019,216	1,019,215,872,000	4.0%	40,769	40,768,634,880	978,447
5	1.5-4M	800,000	2,887,776	2,310,220,944,000	5.0%	144,389	115,511,047,200	2,743,387
6	4-5M	140,000	4,196,365	587,491,128,806	6.0%	251,782	35,249,467,728	3,944,583
7	5-6.5M	0	0	0	8.0%	0	0	0
8	6.5-15M	25,000	8,101,523	202,538,070,000	10.0%	810,152	20,253,807,000	7,291,371
9	15-35M	12,000	18,512,596	222,151,149,158	12.0%	2,221,511	26,658,137,899	16,291,084
10	35-65M	10,000	28,542,965	285,429,650,688	16.0%	4,566,874	45,668,744,110	23,976,091
11	65-135M	11,000	58,687,292	645,560,213,760	20.0%	11,737,458	129,112,042,752	46,949,834
12	135-185M	1,300	80,311,762	104,405,291,172	30.0%	24,093,529	31,321,587,352	56,218,234
13	185-260M	0	0	0	32.0%	0	0	0
14	260-400M	500	130,199,870	65,099,934,900	35.0%	45,569,954	22,784,977,215	84,629,915
15	400-500M	0	0	0	38.0%	0	0	0
16	500-900M	125	255,492,468	31,936,558,500	40.0%	102,196,987	12,774,623,400	153,295,481
17	900-1.2B	0	0	0	43.0%	0	0	0
18	1.2B-3.0B	75	669,866,652	50,239,998,900	45.0%	301,439,993	22,607,999,505	368,426,659
19	3.0-7B	0	0	0	48.0%	0	0	0
20	7 Bil or more	0	0	0	50.0%	0	0	0
Total		100,000,000		18,909,183,050,385			612,189,672,646	
							paid into U.S. Treasury	

Amortization Plan A, year 6

NET WORTH TAX TABLE for 1999 (payable by 4/15/00)

Plan A - Based on 100% maximum proposed amortization rate

Note: These data are projected from the same sources as shown on Distribution of Wealth Graph, p36, and Appendix II, and do not indicate household yearly increases or decreases except for Net Worth Taxes paid. Tables for subsequent years follow on sequential pages. All tables are summarized page 51-53.

Bracket	Household Net Worth dollars	Number of Households	end 1999 per Household av Net Worth dollars	end 1999 Bracket Group Net Worth dollars	NW Tax yearly percent	Pay by 4/15/00 Net Worth Tax Av Household dollars	Pay by 4/15/00 Bracket Group Net Worth Tax dollars	After 4/15/00 per Household av Net Worth dollars
0	under 150K	80,000,000	100,000	8,000,000,000,000	0.0%	0	0	100,000
1	150-200K	10,000,000	166,423	1,664,232,587,325	1.0%	1,664	16,642,325,873	164,759
2	200-600K	5,000,000	361,568	1,807,841,593,600	2.0%	7,231	36,156,831,872	354,337
3	600-800K	3,000,000	601,114	1,803,341,453,970	3.0%	18,033	54,100,243,619	583,080
4	800K-1.5M	1,000,000	978,447	978,447,237,120	4.0%	39,138	39,137,889,485	939,309
5	1.5-4M	800,000	2,743,387	2,194,709,896,800	5.0%	137,169	109,735,494,840	2,606,218
6	4-5M	140,000	3,944,583	552,241,661,078	6.0%	236,675	33,134,499,665	3,707,908
7	5-6.5M	0	0	0	8.0%	0	0	0
8	6.5-15M	25,000	7,291,371	182,284,263,000	10.0%	729,137	18,228,426,300	6,562,233
9	15-35M	22,000	20,133,587	442,938,924,223	12.0%	2,416,030	53,152,670,907	17,717,557
10	35-65M	0	0	0	16.0%	0	0	0
11	65-135M	12,300	51,584,034	634,483,614,731	20.0%	10,316,807	126,896,722,946	41,267,227
12	135-185M	0	0	0	30.0%	0	0	0
13	185-260M	500	84,629,915	42,314,957,685	32.0%	27,081,573	13,540,786,459	57,548,342
14	260-400M	0	0	0	35.0%	0	0	0
15	400-500M	125	153,295,481	19,161,935,100	38.0%	58,252,283	7,281,535,338	95,043,198
16	500-900M	0	0	0	40.0%	0	0	0
17	900-1.2B	0	0	0	43.0%	0	0	0
18	1.2B-3.0B	75	368,426,659	27,631,999,395	45.0%	165,791,996	12,434,399,728	202,634,662
19	3.0-7B	0	0	0	48.0%	0	0	0
20	7 Bil or more	0	0	0	50.0%	0	0	0
Total		100,000,000		18,349,630,124,028			520,441,827,032	
							paid into U.S. Treasury	

Amortization Plan B, year 1

NET WORTH TAX TABLE for 1994 (payable by 4/15/95)

Plan B - Based on 75% of maximum proposed amortization rate

Note: These data are projected from the same sources as shown on Distribution of Wealth Graph, p36, and Appendix II, and do not indicate household yearly increases or decreases except for Net Worth Taxes paid. Tables for subsequent years follow on sequential pages. All tables are summarized pages 51-53.

Bracket	Household Net Worth dollars	Number of Households	end 1994 per Household av Net Worth dollars	end 1994 Bracket Group Net Worth dollars	NW Tax yearly percent	Pay by 4/15/95 Net Worth Tax Av Household dollars	Pay by 4/15/95 Bracket Group Net Worth Tax dollars	After 4/15/95 per Household av Net Worth dollars
0	under 150K	80,000,000	100,000	8,000,000,000,000	0.0%	0	0	100,000
1	150-200K	10,000,000	175,000	1,750,000,000,000	0.7%	1,225	12,250,000,000	173,775
2	200-600K	5,000,000	400,000	2,000,000,000,000	1.4%	5,600	28,000,000,000	394,400
3	600-800K	3,000,000	700,000	2,100,000,000,000	2.1%	14,700	44,100,000,000	685,300
4	800K-1.5M	1,000,000	1,200,000	1,200,000,000,000	2.8%	33,600	33,600,000,000	1,166,400
5	1.5-4M	500,000	3,600,000	1,800,000,000,000	3.5%	126,000	63,000,000,000	3,474,000
6	4-5M	300,000	3,528,000	1,058,400,000,000	4.2%	148,176	44,452,800,000	3,379,824
7	5-6.5M	140,000	5,733,000	802,620,000,000	5.6%	321,048	44,946,720,000	5,411,952
8	6.5-15M	25,000	12,348,000	308,700,000,000	7.0%	864,360	21,609,000,000	11,483,640
9	15-35M	12,000	30,870,000	370,440,000,000	8.4%	2,593,080	31,116,960,000	28,276,920
10	35-65M	10,000	57,330,000	573,300,000,000	11.2%	6,420,960	64,209,600,000	50,909,040
11	65-135M	7,000	114,660,000	802,620,000,000	14.0%	16,052,400	112,366,800,000	98,607,600
12	135-185M	3,000	176,400,000	529,200,000,000	21.0%	37,044,000	111,132,000,000	139,356,000
13	185-260M	1,000	255,780,000	255,780,000,000	22.4%	57,294,720	57,294,720,000	198,485,280
14	260-400M	900	352,800,000	317,520,000,000	24.5%	86,436,000	77,792,400,000	266,364,000
15	400-500M	400	467,460,000	186,984,000,000	26.6%	124,344,360	49,737,744,000	343,115,640
16	500-900M	320	705,600,000	225,792,000,000	28.0%	197,568,000	63,221,760,000	508,032,000
17	900-1.2B	180	1,146,600,000	206,388,000,000	30.1%	345,126,600	62,122,788,000	801,473,400
18	1.2B-3.0B	125	2,469,600,000	308,700,000,000	31.5%	777,924,000	97,240,500,000	1,691,676,000
19	3.0-7B	60	6,174,000,000	370,440,000,000	33.6%	2,074,464,000	124,467,840,000	4,099,536,000
20	7 Bil or more	15	12,348,000,000	185,220,000,000	35.0%	4,321,800,000	64,827,000,000	8,026,200,000
Total		100,000,000		23,352,104,000,000			1,207,488,632,000	
							paid into U.S. Treasury	

Amortization Plan B, year 2

NET WORTH TAX TABLE for 1995 (payable by 4/15/96)

Plan B - Based on 75% of maximum proposed amortization rate

Note: These data are projected from the same sources as shown on Distribution of Wealth Graph, p36, and Appendix II, and do not indicate household yearly increases or decreases except for Net Worth Taxes paid. Tables for subsequent years follow on sequential pages. All tables are summarized pages 51-53.

Bracket	Household Net Worth dollars	Number of Households	end 1995 per Household av Net Worth dollars	end 1995 Bracket Group Net Worth dollars	NW Tax yearly percent	Pay by 4/15/96 Net Worth Tax Av Household dollars	Pay by 4/15/96 Bracket Group Net Worth Tax dollars	After 4/15/96 per Household av Net Worth dollars
0	under 150K	80,000,000	100,000	8,000,000,000,000	0.0%	0	0	100,000
1	150-200K	10,000,000	173,775	1,737,750,000,000	0.7%	1,216	12,164,250,000	172,559
2	200-600K	5,000,000	394,400	1,972,000,000,000	1.4%	5,522	27,608,000,000	388,878
3	600-800K	3,000,000	685,300	2,055,900,000,000	2.1%	14,391	43,173,900,000	670,909
4	800K-1.5M	1,000,000	1,166,400	1,166,400,000,000	2.8%	32,659	32,659,200,000	1,133,741
5	1.5-4M	800,000	3,426,912	2,741,529,600,000	3.5%	119,942	95,953,536,000	3,306,970
6	4-5M	0	0	0	4.2%	0	0	0
7	5-6.5M	140,000	5,411,952	757,673,280,000	5.6%	303,069	42,429,703,680	5,108,883
8	6.5-15M	25,000	11,483,640	287,091,000,000	7.0%	803,855	20,096,370,000	10,679,785
9	15-35M	12,000	28,276,920	339,323,040,000	8.4%	2,375,261	28,503,135,360	25,901,659
10	35-65M	10,000	50,909,040	509,090,400,000	11.2%	5,701,812	57,018,124,800	45,207,228
11	65-135M	7,000	98,607,600	690,253,200,000	14.0%	13,805,064	96,635,448,000	84,802,536
12	135-185M	3,000	139,356,000	418,068,000,000	21.0%	29,264,760	87,794,280,000	110,091,240
13	185-260M	1,000	198,485,280	198,485,280,000	22.4%	44,460,703	44,460,702,720	154,024,577
14	260-400M	1,300	304,739,820	396,161,766,000	24.5%	74,661,256	97,059,632,670	230,078,564
15	400-500M	0	0	0	26.6%	0	0	0
16	500-900M	500	654,752,700	327,376,350,000	28.0%	183,330,756	91,665,378,000	471,421,944
17	900-1.2B	0	0	0	30.1%	0	0	0
18	1.2B-3.0B	125	1,691,676,000	211,459,500,000	31.5%	532,877,940	66,609,742,500	1,158,798,060
19	3.0-7B	60	4,099,536,000	245,972,160,000	33.6%	1,377,444,096	82,646,645,760	2,722,091,904
20	7 Bil or more	15	8,026,200,000	120,393,000,000	35.0%	2,809,170,000	42,137,550,000	5,217,030,000
Total		100,000,000		22,174,926,576,000			968,615,599,490	
							paid into U.S. Treasury	

Amortization Plan B, year 3

NET WORTH TAX TABLE for 1996 (payable by 4/15/97)

Plan B - Based on 75% of maximum proposed amortization rate

Note: These data are projected from the same sources as shown on Distribution of Wealth Graph, p36, and Appendix II, and do not indicate household yearly increases or decreases except for Net Worth Taxes paid. Tables for subsequent years follow on sequential pages. All tables are summarized pages 51-53.

Bracket	Household Net Worth dollars	Number of Households	end 1996 per Household av Net Worth dollars	end 1996 Bracket Group Net Worth dollars	NW Tax yearly percent	Pay by 4/15/97 Net Worth Tax Av Household dollars	Pay by 4/15/97 Bracket Group Net Worth Tax dollars	After 4/15/97 per Household av Net Worth dollars
0	under 150K	80,000,000	100,000	8,000,000,000,000	0.0%	0	0	100,000
1	150-200K	10,000,000	172,559	1,725,585,750,000	0.7%	1,208	12,079,100,250	171,351
2	200-600K	5,000,000	388,878	1,944,392,000,000	1.4%	5,444	27,221,488,000	383,434
3	600-800K	3,000,000	670,909	2,012,726,100,000	2.1%	14,089	42,267,248,100	656,820
4	800K-1.5M	1,000,000	1,133,741	1,133,740,800,000	2.8%	31,745	31,744,742,400	1,101,996
5	1.5-4M	800,000	3,306,970	2,645,576,064,000	3.5%	115,744	92,595,162,240	3,191,226
6	4-5M	0	0	0	4.2%	0	0	0
7	5-6.5M	140,000	5,108,883	715,243,576,320	5.6%	286,097	40,053,640,274	4,822,785
8	6.5-15M	25,000	10,679,785	266,994,630,000	7.0%	747,585	18,689,624,100	9,932,200
9	15-35M	12,000	25,901,659	310,819,904,640	8.4%	2,175,739	26,108,871,990	23,725,919
10	35-65M	10,000	45,207,228	452,072,275,200	11.2%	5,063,209	50,632,094,822	40,144,018
11	65-135M	10,000	97,446,888	974,468,880,000	14.0%	13,642,564	136,425,643,200	83,804,324
12	135-185M	1,000	154,024,577	154,024,577,280	21.0%	32,345,161	32,345,161,229	121,679,416
13	185-260M	1,300	230,078,564	299,102,133,330	22.4%	51,537,598	66,998,877,866	178,540,966
14	260-400M	0	0	0	24.5%	0	0	0
15	400-500M	500	471,421,944	235,710,972,000	26.6%	125,398,237	62,699,118,552	346,023,707
16	500-900M	0	0	0	28.0%	0	0	0
17	900-1.2B	125	1,158,798,060	144,849,757,500	30.1%	348,798,216	43,599,777,008	809,999,844
18	1.2B-3.0B	60	2,722,091,904	163,325,514,240	31.5%	857,458,950	51,447,536,986	1,864,632,954
19	3.0-7B	15	5,217,030,000	78,255,450,000	33.6%	1,752,922,080	26,293,831,200	3,464,107,920
20	7 Bil or more	0	0	0	35.0%	0	0	0
Total		100,000,000		21,256,888,384,510			761,201,918,216	
							paid into U.S. Treasury	

Amortization Plan B, year 4

NET WORTH TAX TABLE for 1997 (payable by 4/15/98)

Plan B - Based on 75% of maximum proposed amortization rate

Note: These data are projected from the same sources as shown on Distribution of Wealth Graph, p36, and Appendix II, and do not indicate household yearly increases or decreases except for Net Worth Taxes paid.
Tables for subsequent years follow on sequential pages. All tables are summarized pages 51-53.

Bracket	Household Net Worth dollars	Number of Households	end 1997 per Household av Net Worth dollars	end 1997 Bracket Group Net Worth dollars	NW Tax yearly percent	Pay by 4/15/98 Net Worth Tax Av Household dollars	Pay by 4/15/98 Bracket Group Net Worth Tax dollars	After 4/15/98 per Household av Net Worth dollars
0	under 150K	80,000,000	100,000	8,000,000,000,000	0.0%	0	0	100,000
1	150-200K	10,000,000	171,351	1,713,506,649,750	0.7%	1,199	11,994,546,548	170,151
2	200-600K	5,000,000	383,434	1,917,170,512,000	1.4%	5,368	26,840,387,168	378,066
3	600-800K	3,000,000	656,820	1,970,458,851,900	2.1%	13,793	41,379,635,890	643,026
4	800K-1.5M	1,000,000	1,101,996	1,101,996,057,600	2.8%	30,856	30,855,889,613	1,071,140
5	1.5-4M	800,000	3,191,226	2,552,980,901,760	3.5%	111,693	89,354,331,562	3,079,533
6	4-5M	140,000	4,822,785	675,189,936,046	4.2%	202,557	28,357,977,314	4,620,228
7	5-6.5M	0	0	0	5.6%	0	0	0
8	6.5-15M	25,000	9,932,200	248,305,005,900	7.0%	695,254	17,381,350,413	9,236,946
9	15-35M	12,000	23,725,919	284,711,032,650	8.4%	1,992,977	23,915,726,743	21,732,942
10	35-65M	10,000	40,144,018	401,440,180,378	11.2%	4,496,130	44,961,300,202	35,647,888
11	65-135M	11,000	102,741,870	1,130,160,568,522	14.0%	14,383,862	158,222,479,593	88,358,008
12	135-185M	1,300	178,540,966	232,103,255,464	21.0%	37,493,603	48,741,683,647	141,047,363
13	185-260M	0	0	0	22.4%	0	0	0
14	260-400M	500	346,023,707	173,011,853,448	24.5%	84,775,808	42,387,904,095	261,247,899
15	400-500M	0	0	0	26.6%	0	0	0
16	500-900M	125	809,999,844	101,249,980,493	28.0%	226,799,956	28,349,994,538	583,199,888
17	900-1.2B	0	0	0	30.1%	0	0	0
18	1.2B-3.0B	60	1,864,632,954	111,877,977,254	31.5%	587,359,381	35,241,562,835	1,277,273,574
19	3.0-7B	15	3,464,107,920	51,961,618,800	33.6%	1,163,940,261	17,459,103,917	2,300,167,659
20	7 Bil or more	0	0	0	35.0%	0	0	0
Total		100,000,000		20,666,124,381,965			645,443,874,077	
							paid into U.S. Treasury	

Amortization Plan B, year 5

NET WORTH TAX TABLE for 1998 (payable by 4/15/99)

Plan B - Based on 75% of maximum proposed amortization rate

Note: These data are projected from the same sources as shown on Distribution of Wealth Graph, p36, and Appendix II, and do not indicate household yearly increases or decreases except for Net Worth Taxes paid. Tables for subsequent years follow on sequential pages. All tables are summarized pages 51-53.

Bracket	Household Net Worth dollars	Number of Households	end 1998 per Household av Net Worth dollars	end 1998 Bracket Group Net Worth dollars	NW Tax yearly percent	Pay by 4/15/99 Net Worth Tax Av Household dollars	Pay by 4/15/99 Bracket Group Net Worth Tax dollars	After 4/15/99 per Household av Net Worth dollars
0	under 150K	80,000,000	100,000	8,000,000,000,000	0.0%	0	0	100,000
1	150-200K	10,000,000	170,151	1,701,512,103,202	0.7%	1,191	11,910,584,722	168,960
2	200-600K	5,000,000	378,066	1,890,330,124,832	1.4%	5,293	26,464,621,748	372,773
3	600-800K	3,000,000	643,026	1,929,079,216,010	2.1%	13,504	40,510,663,536	629,523
4	800K-1.5M	1,000,000	1,071,140	1,071,140,167,987	2.8%	29,992	29,991,924,704	1,041,148
5	1.5-4M	800,000	3,079,533	2,463,626,570,198	3.5%	107,784	86,226,929,957	2,971,750
6	4-5M	140,000	4,620,228	646,831,958,732	4.2%	194,050	27,166,942,267	4,426,179
7	5-6.5M	0	0	0	5.6%	0	0	0
8	6.5-15M	25,000	9,236,946	230,923,655,487	7.0%	646,586	16,164,655,884	8,590,360
9	15-35M	12,000	21,732,942	260,795,305,908	8.4%	1,825,567	21,906,805,696	19,907,375
10	35-65M	10,000	35,647,888	356,478,880,175	11.2%	3,992,563	39,925,634,580	31,655,325
11	65-135M	11,000	88,358,008	971,938,088,929	14.0%	12,370,121	136,071,332,450	75,987,887
12	135-185M	1,300	141,047,363	183,361,571,817	21.0%	29,619,946	38,505,930,081	111,427,417
13	185-260M	0	0	0	22.4%	0	0	0
14	260-400M	500	261,247,899	130,623,949,353	24.5%	64,005,735	32,002,867,592	197,242,164
15	400-500M	0	0	0	26.6%	0	0	0
16	500-900M	125	583,199,888	72,899,985,955	28.0%	163,295,969	20,411,996,067	419,903,919
17	900-1.2B	0	0	0	30.1%	0	0	0
18	1.2B-3.0B	75	1,788,720,616	134,154,046,220	31.5%	563,446,994	42,258,524,559	1,225,273,622
19	3.0-7B	0	0	0	33.6%	0	0	0
20	7 Bil or more	0	0	0	35.0%	0	0	0
Total		100,000,000		20,043,695,624,805			569,519,413,843	
							paid into U.S. Treasury	

Amortization Plan B, year 6

NET WORTH TAX TABLE for 1999 (payable by 4/15/00)

Plan B - Based on 75% of maximum proposed amortization rate

Note: These data are projected from the same sources as shown on Distribution of Wealth Graph, p36, and Appendix II, and do not indicate household yearly increases or decreases except for Net Worth Taxes paid.
Tables for subsequent years follow on sequential pages. All tables are summarized pages 51-53.

Bracket	Household Net Worth dollars	Number of Households	end 1999 per Household av Net Worth dollars	end 1999 Bracket Group Net Worth dollars	NW Tax yearly percent	Pay by 4/15/00 Net Worth Tax Av Household dollars	Pay by 4/15/00 Bracket Group Net Worth Tax dollars	After 4/15/00 per Household av Net Worth dollars
0	under 150K	80,000,000	100,000	8,000,000,000,000	0.0%	0	0	100,000
1	150-200K	10,000,000	168,960	1,689,601,518,479	0.7%	1,183	11,827,210,629	167,777
2	200-600K	5,000,000	372,773	1,863,865,503,084	1.4%	5,219	26,094,117,043	367,554
3	600-800K	3,000,000	629,523	1,888,568,552,474	2.1%	13,220	39,659,939,602	616,303
4	800K-1.5M	1,000,000	1,041,148	1,041,148,243,284	2.8%	29,152	29,152,150,812	1,011,996
5	1.5-4M	800,000	2,971,750	2,377,399,640,241	3.5%	104,011	83,208,987,408	2,867,738
6	4-5M	140,000	4,426,179	619,665,016,465	4.2%	185,900	26,025,930,692	4,240,279
7	5-6.5M	0	0	0	5.6%	0	0	0
8	6.5-15M	25,000	8,590,360	214,758,999,603	7.0%	601,325	15,033,129,972	7,989,035
9	15-35M	22,000	25,781,350	567,189,695,349	8.4%	2,165,633	47,643,934,409	23,615,716
10	35-65M	0	0	0	11.2%	0	0	0
11	65-135M	12,300	93,707,652	1,152,604,117,582	14.0%	13,119,071	161,364,576,462	80,588,581
12	135-185M	0	0	0	21.0%	0	0	0
13	185-260M	500	197,242,164	98,621,081,762	22.4%	44,182,245	22,091,122,315	153,059,919
14	260-400M	0	0	0	24.5%	0	0	0
15	400-500M	125	419,903,919	52,487,989,887	26.6%	111,694,442	13,961,805,310	308,209,477
16	500-900M	0	0	0	28.0%	0	0	0
17	900-1.2B	0	0	0	30.1%	0	0	0
18	1.2B-3.0B	75	1,225,273,622	91,895,521,661	31.5%	385,961,191	28,947,089,323	839,312,431
19	3.0-7B	0	0	0	33.6%	0	0	0
20	7 Bil or more	0	0	0	35.0%	0	0	0
Total		100,000,000		19,657,805,879,872			505,009,993,977	
							paid into U.S. Treasury	

Amortization Plan B, year 7

NET WORTH TAX TABLE for 2000 (payable by 4/15/01)

Plan B - Based on 75% of maximum proposed amortization rate

Note: These data are projected from the same sources as shown on Distribution of Wealth Graph, p36, and Appendix II, and do not indicate household yearly increases or decreases except for Net Worth Taxes paid. Tables for subsequent years follow on sequential pages. All tables are summarized pages 51-53.

Bracket	Household Net Worth dollars	Number of Households	end 2000 per Household av Net Worth dollars	end 2000 Bracket Group Net Worth dollars	NW Tax yearly percent	Pay by 4/15/01 Net Worth Tax Av Household dollars	Pay by 4/15/01 Bracket Group Net Worth Tax dollars	After 4/15/01 per Household av Net Worth dollars
0	under 150K	80,000,000	100,000	8,000,000,000,000	0.0%	0	0	100,000
1	150-200K	10,000,000	167,777	1,677,774,307,850	0.7%	1,174	11,744,420,155	166,603
2	200-600K	5,000,000	367,554	1,837,771,386,041	1.4%	5,146	25,728,799,405	362,409
3	600-800K	3,000,000	616,303	1,848,908,612,872	2.1%	12,942	38,827,080,870	603,361
4	800K-1.5M	1,000,000	1,011,996	1,011,996,092,472	2.8%	28,336	28,335,890,589	983,660
5	1.5-4M	800,000	2,867,738	2,294,190,652,833	3.5%	100,371	80,296,672,849	2,767,367
6	4-5M	140,000	4,240,279	593,639,085,774	4.2%	178,092	24,932,841,603	4,062,187
7	5-6.5M	0	0	0	5.6%	0	0	0
8	6.5-15M	25,000	7,989,035	199,725,869,631	7.0%	559,232	13,980,810,874	7,429,802
9	15-35M	22,000	23,615,716	519,545,760,940	8.4%	1,983,720	43,641,843,919	21,631,996
10	35-65M	0	0	0	11.2%	0	0	0
11	65-135M	12,300	80,588,581	991,239,541,121	14.0%	11,282,401	138,773,535,757	69,306,179
12	135-185M	0	0	0	21.0%	0	0	0
13	185-260M	500	153,059,919	76,529,959,447	22.4%	34,285,422	17,142,710,916	118,774,497
14	260-400M	0	0	0	24.5%	0	0	0
15	400-500M	125	308,209,477	38,526,184,577	26.6%	81,983,721	10,247,965,098	226,225,756
16	500-900M	0	0	0	28.0%	0	0	0
17	900-1.2B	0	0	0	30.1%	0	0	0
18	1.2B-3.0B	75	839,312,431	62,948,432,338	31.5%	264,383,416	19,828,756,186	574,929,015
19	3.0-7B	0	0	0	33.6%	0	0	0
20	7 Bil or more	0	0	0	35.0%	0	0	0
Total		100,000,000		19,152,795,885,895			453,481,328,221	
							paid into U.S. Treasury	

Amortization Plan B, year 8

NET WORTH TAX TABLE for 2001 (payable by 4/15/02)

Plan B - Based on 75% of maximum proposed amortization rate

Note: These data are projected from the same sources as shown on Distribution of Wealth Graph, p36, and Appendix II, and do not indicate household yearly increases or decreases except for Net Worth Taxes paid.

Tables for subsequent years follow on sequential pages. All tables are summarized pages 51-53.

Bracket	Household Net Worth dollars	Number of Households	end 2001 per Household av Net Worth dollars	end 2001 Bracket Group Net Worth dollars	NW Tax yearly percent	Pay by 4/15/02 Net Worth Tax Av Household dollars	Pay by 4/15/02 Bracket Group Net Worth Tax dollars	After 4/15/02 per Household av Net Worth dollars
0	under 150K	80,000,000	100,000	8,000,000,000,000	0.0%	0	0	100,000
1	150-200K	10,000,000	166,603	1,666,029,887,695	0.7%	1,166	11,662,209,214	165,437
2	200-600K	5,000,000	362,409	1,812,042,586,637	1.4%	5,074	25,368,596,213	357,335
3	600-800K	3,000,000	603,361	1,810,081,532,002	2.1%	12,671	38,011,712,172	590,690
4	800K-1.5M	1,000,000	983,660	983,660,201,882	2.8%	27,542	27,542,485,653	956,118
5	1.5-4M	800,000	2,767,367	2,213,893,979,984	3.5%	96,858	77,486,289,299	2,670,510
6	4-5M	140,000	4,062,187	568,706,244,171	4.2%	170,612	23,885,662,255	3,891,576
7	5-6.5M	0	0	0	5.6%	0	0	0
8	6.5-15M	25,000	7,429,802	185,745,058,757	7.0%	520,086	13,002,154,113	6,909,716
9	15-35M	22,000	21,631,996	475,903,917,021	8.4%	1,817,088	39,975,929,030	19,814,909
10	35-65M	0	0	0	11.2%	0	0	0
11	65-135M	12,800	94,040,338	1,203,716,328,702	14.0%	13,165,647	168,520,286,018	80,874,691
12	135-185M	0	0	0	21.0%	0	0	0
13	185-260M	0	0	0	22.4%	0	0	0
14	260-400M	125	226,225,756	28,278,219,480	24.5%	55,425,310	6,928,163,773	170,800,446
15	400-500M	0	0	0	26.6%	0	0	0
16	500-900M	75	574,929,015	43,119,676,151	28.0%	160,980,124	12,073,509,322	413,948,891
17	900-1.2B	0	0	0	30.1%	0	0	0
18	1.2B-3.0B	0	0	0	31.5%	0	0	0
19	3.0-7B	0	0	0	33.6%	0	0	0
20	7 Bil or more	0	0	0	35.0%	0	0	0
Total		100,000,000		18,991,177,632,482			444,456,997,062	
							paid into U.S. Treasury	

Amortization Plan B, year 8

NET WORTH TAX TABLE for 2002 (payable by 4/15/03)

Plan B - Based on 75% of maximum proposed amortization rate

Note: These data are projected from the same sources as shown on Distribution of Wealth Graph, p36, and Appendix II, and do not indicate household yearly increases or decreases except for Net Worth Taxes paid.
Tables for subsequent years follow on sequential pages. All tables are summarized pages 51-53.

Bracket	Household Net Worth dollars	Number of Households	end 2002 per Household av Net Worth dollars	end 2002 Bracket Group Net Worth dollars	NW Tax yearly percent	Pay by 4/15/03 Net Worth Tax Av Household dollars	Pay by 4/15/03 Bracket Group Net Worth Tax dollars	After 4/15/03 per Household av Net Worth dollars
0	under 150K	80,000,000	100,000	8,000,000,000,000	0.0%	0	0	100,000
1	150-200K	10,000,000	165,437	1,654,367,678,481	0.7%	1,158	11,580,573,749	164,279
2	200-600K	8,000,000	474,012	3,792,098,952,112	1.4%	6,636	53,089,385,330	467,376
3	600-800K	0	0	0	2.1%	0	0	0
4	800K-1.5M	1,000,000	956,118	956,117,716,230	2.8%	26,771	26,771,296,054	929,346
5	1.5-4M	940,000	3,281,043	3,084,180,043,281	3.5%	114,836	107,946,301,515	3,166,206
6	4-5M	0	0	0	4.2%	0	0	0
7	5-6.5M	0	0	0	5.6%	0	0	0
8	6.5-15M	25,000	6,909,716	172,742,904,644	7.0%	483,680	12,092,003,325	6,426,036
9	15-35M	22,000	19,814,909	435,927,987,991	8.4%	1,664,452	36,617,950,991	18,150,456
10	35-65M	0	0	0	11.2%	0	0	0
11	65-135M	12,800	80,874,691	1,035,196,042,684	14.0%	11,322,457	144,927,445,976	69,552,234
12	135-185M	125	170,800,446	21,350,055,707	21.0%	35,868,094	4,483,511,699	134,932,352
13	185-260M	0	0	0	22.4%	0	0	0
14	260-400M	0	0	0	24.5%	0	0	0
15	400-500M	75	413,948,891	31,046,166,829	26.6%	110,110,405	8,258,280,376	303,838,486
16	500-900M	0	0	0	28.0%	0	0	0
17	900-1.2B	0	0	0	30.1%	0	0	0
18	1.2B-3.0B	0	0	0	31.5%	0	0	0
19	3.0-7B	0	0	0	33.6%	0	0	0
20	7 Bil or more	0	0	0	35.0%	0	0	0
Total		100,000,000		19,183,027,547,959			405,766,749,015	
							paid into U.S. Treasury	

Amortization Plan B, year 10

NET WORTH TAX TABLE for 2003 (payable by 4/15/04)

Plan B - Based on 75% of maximum proposed amortization rate

Note: These data are projected from the same sources as shown on Distribution of Wealth Graph, p36, and Appendix II, and do not indicate household yearly increases or decreases except for Net Worth Taxes paid.
Tables for subsequent years follow on sequential pages. All tables are summarized pages 51-53.

Bracket	Household Net Worth dollars	Number of Households	end 2003 per Household av Net Worth dollars	end 2003 Bracket Group Net Worth dollars	NW Tax yearly percent	Pay by 4/15/04 Net Worth Tax Av Household dollars	Pay by 4/15/04 Bracket Group Net Worth Tax dollars	After 4/15/04 per Household av Net Worth dollars
0	under 150K	80,000,000	100,000	8,000,000,000,000	0.0%	0	0	100,000
1	150-200K	10,000,000	164,279	1,642,787,104,732	0.7%	1,150	11,499,509,733	163,129
2	200-600K	8,000,000	467,376	3,739,009,566,782	1.4%	6,543	52,346,133,935	460,833
3	600-800K	0	0	0	2.1%	0	0	0
4	800K-1.5M	1,000,000	929,346	929,346,420,175	2.8%	26,022	26,021,699,765	903,325
5	1.5-4M	940,000	3,166,206	2,976,233,741,766	3.5%	110,817	104,168,180,962	3,055,389
6	4-5M	0	0	0	4.2%	0	0	0
7	5-6.5M	25,000	6,426,036	160,650,901,319	5.6%	359,858	8,996,450,474	6,066,178
8	6.5-15M	0	0	0	7.0%	0	0	0
9	15-35M	22,000	18,150,456	399,310,037,000	8.4%	1,524,638	33,542,043,108	16,625,818
10	35-65M	0	0	0	11.2%	0	0	0
11	65-135M	12,925	102,242,293	1,321,481,638,235	14.0%	14,313,921	185,007,429,353	87,928,372
12	135-185M	0	0	0	21.0%	0	0	0
13	185-260M	0	0	0	22.4%	0	0	0
14	260-400M	75	303,838,486	22,787,886,452	24.5%	74,440,429	5,583,032,181	229,398,057
15	400-500M	0	0	0	26.6%	0	0	0
16	500-900M	0	0	0	28.0%	0	0	0
17	900-1.2B	0	0	0	30.1%	0	0	0
18	1.2B-3.0B	0	0	0	31.5%	0	0	0
19	3.0-7B	0	0	0	33.6%	0	0	0
20	7 Bil or more	0	0	0	35.0%	0	0	0
Total		100,000,000		19,191,607,296,462			427,164,479,510	
							paid into U.S. Treasury	

Amortization Plan C, year 1

NET WORTH TAX TABLE for 1994 (payable by 4/15/95)

Plan C - Based on 50% of maximum proposed amortization rate

Note: These data are projected from the same sources as shown on Distribution of Wealth Graph, p. 36, and Appendix II, and do not indicate household yearly increases or decreases except for Net Worth Taxes paid. Tables for subsequent years follow on sequential pages. All tables are summarized page 51-53.

Bracket	Household Net Worth dollars	Number of Households	end 1994 per Household av Net Worth dollars	end 1994 Bracket Group Net Worth dollars	NW Tax yearly percent	Pay by 4/15/95 Net Worth Tax Av Household dollars	Pay by 4/15/95 Bracket Group Net Worth Tax dollars	After 4/15/95 per Household av Net Worth dollars
0	under 150K	80,000,000	100,000	8,000,000,000,000	0.0%	0	0	100,000
1	150-200K	10,000,000	175,000	1,750,000,000,000	0.5%	875	8,750,000,000	174,125
2	200-600K	5,000,000	400,000	2,000,000,000,000	1.0%	4,000	20,000,000,000	396,000
3	600-800K	3,000,000	700,000	2,100,000,000,000	1.5%	10,500	31,500,000,000	689,500
4	800K-1.5M	1,000,000	1,200,000	1,200,000,000,000	2.0%	24,000	24,000,000,000	1,176,000
5	1.5-4M	500,000	3,600,000	1,800,000,000,000	2.5%	90,000	45,000,000,000	3,510,000
6	4-5M	300,000	3,528,000	1,058,400,000,000	3.0%	105,840	31,752,000,000	3,422,160
7	5-6.5M	140,000	5,733,000	802,620,000,000	4.0%	229,320	32,104,800,000	5,503,680
8	6.5-15M	25,000	12,348,000	308,700,000,000	5.0%	617,400	15,435,000,000	11,730,600
9	15-35M	12,000	30,870,000	370,440,000,000	6.0%	1,852,200	22,226,400,000	29,017,800
10	35-65M	10,000	57,330,000	573,300,000,000	8.0%	4,586,400	45,864,000,000	52,743,600
11	65-135M	7,000	114,660,000	802,620,000,000	10.0%	11,466,000	80,262,000,000	103,194,000
12	135-185M	3,000	176,400,000	529,200,000,000	15.0%	26,460,000	79,380,000,000	149,940,000
13	185-260M	1,000	255,780,000	255,780,000,000	16.0%	40,924,800	40,924,800,000	214,855,200
14	260-400M	900	352,800,000	317,520,000,000	17.5%	61,740,000	55,566,000,000	291,060,000
15	400-500M	400	467,460,000	186,984,000,000	19.0%	88,817,400	35,526,960,000	378,642,600
16	500-900M	320	705,600,000	225,792,000,000	20.0%	141,120,000	45,158,400,000	564,480,000
17	900-1.2B	180	1,146,600,000	206,388,000,000	21.5%	246,519,000	44,373,420,000	900,081,000
18	1.2B-3.0B	125	2,469,600,000	308,700,000,000	22.5%	555,660,000	69,457,500,000	1,913,940,000
19	3.0-7B	60	6,174,000,000	370,440,000,000	24.0%	1,481,760,000	88,905,600,000	4,692,240,000
20	7 Bil or more	15	12,348,000,000	185,220,000,000	25.0%	3,087,000,000	46,305,000,000	9,261,000,000
Total		100,000,000		23,352,104,000,000			862,491,880,000	
							paid into U.S. Treasury	

Amortization Plan C, year 2

NET WORTH TAX TABLE for 1995 (payable by 4/15/96)

Plan C - Based on 50% of maximum proposed amortization rate

Note: These data are projected from the same sources as shown on Distribution of Wealth Graph, p. 36, and Appendix II, and do not indicate household yearly increases or decreases except for Net Worth Taxes paid. Tables for subsequent years follow on sequential pages. All tables are summarized page 51-53.

Bracket	Household Net Worth dollars	Number of Households	end 1995 per Household av Net Worth dollars	end 1995 Bracket Group Net Worth dollars	NW Tax yearly percent	Pay by 4/15/96 Net Worth Tax Av Household dollars	Pay by 4/15/96 Bracket Group Net Worth Tax dollars	After 4/15/96 per Household av Net Worth dollars
0	under 150K	80,000,000	100,000	8,000,000,000,000	0.0%	0	0	100,000
1	150-200K	10,000,000	174,125	1,741,250,000,000	0.5%	871	8,706,250,000	173,254
2	200-600K	5,000,000	396,000	1,980,000,000,000	1.0%	3,960	19,800,000,000	392,040
3	600-800K	3,000,000	689,500	2,068,500,000,000	1.5%	10,343	31,027,500,000	679,158
4	800K-1.5M	1,000,000	1,176,000	1,176,000,000,000	2.0%	23,520	23,520,000,000	1,152,480
5	1.5-4M	800,000	3,466,080	2,772,864,000,000	2.5%	86,652	69,321,600,000	3,379,428
6	4-5M	0	0	0	3.0%	0	0	0
7	5-6.5M	140,000	5,503,680	770,515,200,000	4.0%	220,147	30,820,608,000	5,283,533
8	6.5-15M	25,000	11,730,600	293,265,000,000	5.0%	586,530	14,663,250,000	11,144,070
9	15-35M	12,000	29,017,800	348,213,600,000	6.0%	1,741,068	20,892,816,000	27,276,732
10	35-65M	10,000	52,743,600	527,436,000,000	8.0%	4,219,488	42,194,880,000	48,524,112
11	65-135M	7,000	103,194,000	722,358,000,000	10.0%	10,319,400	72,235,800,000	92,874,600
12	135-185M	3,000	149,940,000	449,820,000,000	15.0%	22,491,000	67,473,000,000	127,449,000
13	185-260M	1,000	214,855,200	214,855,200,000	16.0%	34,376,832	34,376,832,000	180,478,368
14	260-400M	1,300	334,851,300	435,306,690,000	17.5%	58,598,978	76,178,670,750	276,252,323
15	400-500M	0	0	0	19.0%	0	0	0
16	500-900M	320	564,480,000	180,633,600,000	20.0%	112,896,000	36,126,720,000	451,584,000
17	900-1.2B	180	900,081,000	162,014,580,000	21.5%	193,517,415	34,833,134,700	706,563,585
18	1.2B-3.0B	125	1,913,940,000	239,242,500,000	22.5%	430,636,500	53,829,562,500	1,483,303,500
19	3.0-7B	60	4,692,240,000	281,534,400,000	24.0%	1,126,137,600	67,568,256,000	3,566,102,400
20	7 Bil or more	15	9,261,000,000	138,915,000,000	25.0%	2,315,250,000	34,728,750,000	6,945,750,000
Total		100,000,000		22,502,723,770,000			738,297,629,950	
							paid into U.S. Treasury	

Amortization Plan C, year 3

NET WORTH TAX TABLE for 1996 (payable by 4/15/97)

Plan C - Based on 50% of maximum proposed amortization rate

Note: These data are projected from the same sources as shown on Distribution of Wealth Graph, p. 36, and Appendix II, and do not indicate household yearly increases or decreases except for Net Worth Taxes paid. Tables for subsequent years follow on sequential pages. All tables are summarized page 51-53.

Bracket	Household Net Worth dollars	Number of Households	end 1996 per Household av Net Worth dollars	end 1996 Bracket Group Net Worth dollars	NW Tax yearly percent	Pay by 4/15/97 Net Worth Tax Av Household dollars	Pay by 4/15/97 Bracket Group Net Worth Tax dollars	After 4/15/97 per Household av Net Worth dollars
0	under 150K	80,000,000	100,000	8,000,000,000,000	0.0%	0	0	100,000
1	150-200K	10,000,000	173,254	1,732,543,750,000	0.5%	866	8,662,718,750	172,388
2	200-600K	5,000,000	392,040	1,960,200,000,000	1.0%	3,920	19,602,000,000	388,120
3	600-800K	3,000,000	679,158	2,037,472,500,000	1.5%	10,187	30,562,087,500	668,970
4	800K-1.5M	1,000,000	1,152,480	1,152,480,000,000	2.0%	23,050	23,049,600,000	1,129,430
5	1.5-4M	800,000	3,379,428	2,703,542,400,000	2.5%	84,486	67,588,560,000	3,294,942
6	4-5M	0	0	0	3.0%	0	0	0
7	5-6.5M	140,000	5,283,533	739,694,592,000	4.0%	211,341	29,587,783,680	5,072,191
8	6.5-15M	25,000	11,144,070	278,601,750,000	5.0%	557,204	13,930,087,500	10,586,867
9	15-35M	12,000	27,276,732	327,320,784,000	6.0%	1,636,604	19,639,247,040	25,640,128
10	35-65M	10,000	48,524,112	485,241,120,000	8.0%	3,881,929	38,819,289,600	44,642,183
11	65-135M	10,000	110,161,800	1,101,618,000,000	10.0%	11,016,180	110,161,800,000	99,145,620
12	135-185M	1,000	180,478,368	180,478,368,000	15.0%	27,071,755	27,071,755,200	153,406,613
13	185-260M	0	0	0	16.0%	0	0	0
14	260-400M	1,300	276,252,323	359,128,019,250	17.5%	48,344,156	62,847,403,369	227,908,166
15	400-500M	320	451,584,000	144,506,880,000	19.0%	85,800,960	27,456,307,200	365,783,040
16	500-900M	180	706,563,585	127,181,445,300	20.0%	141,312,717	25,436,289,060	565,250,868
17	900-1.2B	0	0	0	21.5%	0	0	0
18	1.2B-3.0B	125	1,483,303,500	185,412,937,500	22.5%	333,743,288	41,717,910,938	1,149,560,213
19	3.0-7B	60	3,566,102,400	213,966,144,000	24.0%	855,864,576	51,351,874,560	2,710,237,824
20	7 Bil or more	15	6,945,750,000	104,186,250,000	25.0%	1,736,437,500	26,046,562,500	5,209,312,500
Total		100,000,000		21,833,574,940,050			623,531,276,896	
							paid into U.S. Treasury	

Amortization Plan C, year 4

NET WORTH TAX TABLE for 1997 (payable by 4/15/98)

Plan C - Based on 50% of maximum proposed amortization rate

Note: These data are projected from the same sources as shown on Distribution of Wealth Graph, p. 36, and Appendix II, and do not indicate household yearly increases or decreases except for Net Worth Taxes paid. Tables for subsequent years follow on sequential pages. All tables are summarized page 51-53.

Bracket	Household Net Worth dollars	Number of Households	end 1997 per Household av Net Worth dollars	end 1997 Bracket Group Net Worth dollars	NW Tax yearly percent	Pay by 4/15/98 Net Worth Tax Av Household dollars	Pay by 4/15/98 Bracket Group Net Worth Tax dollars	After 4/15/98 per Household av Net Worth dollars
0	under 150K	80,000,000	100,000	8,000,000,000,000	0.0%	0	0	100,000
1	150-200K	10,000,000	172,388	1,723,881,031,250	0.5%	862	8,619,405,156	171,526
2	200-600K	5,000,000	388,120	1,940,598,000,000	1.0%	3,881	19,405,980,000	384,238
3	600-800K	3,000,000	668,970	2,006,910,412,500	1.5%	10,035	30,103,656,188	658,936
4	800K-1.5M	1,000,000	1,129,430	1,129,430,400,000	2.0%	22,589	22,588,608,000	1,106,842
5	1.5-4M	800,000	3,294,942	2,635,953,840,000	2.5%	82,374	65,898,846,000	3,212,569
6	4-5M	0	0	0	3.0%	0	0	0
7	5-6.5M	140,000	5,072,191	710,106,808,320	4.0%	202,888	28,404,272,333	4,869,304
8	6.5-15M	25,000	10,586,867	264,671,662,500	5.0%	529,343	13,233,583,125	10,057,523
9	15-35M	12,000	25,640,128	307,681,536,960	6.0%	1,538,408	18,460,892,218	24,101,720
10	35-65M	10,000	44,642,183	446,421,830,400	8.0%	3,571,375	35,713,746,432	41,070,808
11	65-135M	10,000	99,145,620	991,456,200,000	10.0%	9,914,562	99,145,620,000	89,231,058
12	135-185M	1,000	153,406,613	153,406,612,800	15.0%	23,010,992	23,010,991,920	130,395,621
13	185-260M	1,300	227,908,166	296,280,615,881	16.0%	36,465,307	47,404,898,541	191,442,859
14	260-400M	320	365,783,040	117,050,572,800	17.5%	64,012,032	20,483,850,240	301,771,008
15	400-500M	0	0	0	19.0%	0	0	0
16	500-900M	180	565,250,868	101,745,156,240	20.0%	113,050,174	20,349,031,248	452,200,694
17	900-1.2B	125	1,149,560,213	143,695,026,563	21.5%	247,155,446	30,894,430,711	902,404,767
18	1.2B-3.0B	60	2,710,237,824	162,614,269,440	22.5%	609,803,510	36,588,210,624	2,100,434,314
19	3.0-7B	15	5,209,312,500	78,139,687,500	24.0%	1,250,235,000	18,753,525,000	3,959,077,500
20	7 Bil or more	0	0	0	25.0%	0	0	0
Total		100,000,000		21,210,043,663,154			539,059,547,735	
							paid into U.S. Treasury	

Amortization Plan C, year 5

NET WORTH TAX TABLE for 1998 (payable by 4/15/99)

Plan C - Based on 50% of maximum proposed amortization rate

Note: These data are projected from the same sources as shown on Distribution of Wealth Graph, p. 36, and Appendix II, and do not indicate household yearly increases or decreases except for Net Worth Taxes paid. Tables for subsequent years follow on sequential pages. All tables are summarized page 51-53.

Bracket	Household Net Worth dollars	Number of Households	end 1998 per Household av Net Worth dollars	end 1998 Bracket Group Net Worth dollars	NW Tax yearly percent	Pay by 4/15/99 Net Worth Tax Av Household dollars	Pay by 4/15/99 Bracket Group Net Worth Tax dollars	After 4/15/99 per Household av Net Worth dollars
0	under 150K	80,000,000	100,000	8,000,000,000,000	0.0%	0	0	100,000
1	150-200K	10,000,000	171,526	1,715,261,626,094	0.5%	858	8,576,308,130	170,669
2	200-600K	5,000,000	384,238	1,921,192,020,000	1.0%	3,842	19,211,920,200	380,396
3	600-800K	3,000,000	658,936	1,976,806,756,313	1.5%	9,884	29,652,101,345	649,052
4	800K-1.5M	1,000,000	1,106,842	1,106,841,792,000	2.0%	22,137	22,136,835,840	1,084,705
5	1.5-4M	800,000	3,212,569	2,570,054,994,000	2.5%	80,314	64,251,374,850	3,132,255
6	4-5M	140,000	4,869,304	681,702,535,987	3.0%	146,079	20,451,076,080	4,723,225
7	5-6.5M	0	0	0	4.0%	0	0	0
8	6.5-15M	25,000	10,057,523	251,438,079,375	5.0%	502,876	12,571,903,969	9,554,647
9	15-35M	12,000	24,101,720	289,220,644,742	6.0%	1,446,103	17,353,238,685	22,655,617
10	35-65M	10,000	41,070,808	410,708,083,968	8.0%	3,285,665	32,856,646,717	37,785,144
11	65-135M	11,000	109,813,339	1,207,946,733,840	10.0%	10,981,334	120,794,673,384	98,832,005
12	135-185M	0	0	0	15.0%	0	0	0
13	185-260M	1,300	191,442,859	248,875,717,340	16.0%	30,630,858	39,820,114,774	160,812,002
14	260-400M	320	301,771,008	96,566,722,560	17.5%	52,809,926	16,899,176,448	248,961,082
15	400-500M	180	452,200,694	81,396,124,992	19.0%	85,918,132	15,465,263,748	366,282,562
16	500-900M	0	0	0	20.0%	0	0	0
17	900-1.2B	125	902,404,767	112,800,595,852	21.5%	194,017,025	24,252,128,108	708,387,742
18	1.2B-3.0B	60	2,100,434,314	126,026,058,816	22.5%	472,597,721	28,355,863,234	1,627,836,593
19	3.0-7B	15	3,959,077,500	59,386,162,500	24.0%	950,178,600	14,252,679,000	3,008,898,900
20	7 Bil or more	0	0	0	25.0%	0	0	0
Total		100,000,000		20,856,224,648,379			486,901,304,512	
							paid into U.S. Treasury	

Amortization Plan C, year 6

NET WORTH TAX TABLE for 1999 (payable by 4/15/00)

Plan C - Based on 50% of maximum proposed amortization rate

Note: These data are projected from the same sources as shown on Distribution of Wealth Graph, p. 36, and Appendix II, and do not indicate household yearly increases or decreases except for Net Worth Taxes paid. Tables for subsequent years follow on sequential pages. All tables are summarized page 51-53.

Bracket	Household Net Worth dollars	Number of Households	end 1999 per Household av Net Worth dollars	end 1999 Bracket Group Net Worth dollars	NW Tax yearly percent	Pay by 4/15/00 Net Worth Tax Av Household dollars	Pay by 4/15/00 Bracket Group Net Worth Tax dollars	After 4/15/00 per Household av Net Worth dollars
0	under 150K	80,000,000	100,000	8,000,000,000,000	0.0%	0	0	100,000
1	150-200K	10,000,000	170,669	1,706,685,317,963	0.5%	853	8,533,426,590	169,815
2	200-600K	5,000,000	380,396	1,901,980,099,800	1.0%	3,804	19,019,800,998	376,592
3	600-800K	3,000,000	649,052	1,947,154,654,968	1.5%	9,736	29,207,319,825	639,316
4	800K-1.5M	1,000,000	1,084,705	1,084,704,956,160	2.0%	21,694	21,694,099,123	1,063,011
5	1.5-4M	800,000	3,132,255	2,505,803,619,150	2.5%	78,306	62,645,090,479	3,053,948
6	4-5M	140,000	4,723,225	661,251,459,908	3.0%	141,697	19,837,543,797	4,581,528
7	5-6.5M	0	0	0	4.0%	0	0	0
8	6.5-15M	25,000	9,554,647	238,866,175,406	5.0%	477,732	11,943,308,770	9,076,915
9	15-35M	12,000	22,655,617	271,867,406,058	6.0%	1,359,337	16,312,044,363	21,296,280
10	35-65M	10,000	37,785,144	377,851,437,251	8.0%	3,022,811	30,228,114,980	34,762,332
11	65-135M	11,000	98,832,005	1,087,152,060,456	10.0%	9,883,201	108,715,206,046	88,948,805
12	135-185M	1,300	160,812,002	209,055,602,566	15.0%	24,121,800	31,358,340,385	136,690,202
13	185-260M	320	248,961,082	79,667,546,112	16.0%	39,833,773	12,746,807,378	209,127,309
14	260-400M	180	366,282,562	65,930,861,244	17.5%	64,099,448	11,537,900,718	302,183,114
15	400-500M	0	0	0	19.0%	0	0	0
16	500-900M	125	708,387,742	88,548,467,743	20.0%	141,677,548	17,709,693,549	566,710,194
17	900-1.2B	0	0	0	21.5%	0	0	0
18	1.2B-3.0B	60	1,627,836,593	97,670,195,582	22.5%	366,263,233	21,975,794,006	1,261,573,360
19	3.0-7B	15	3,008,898,900	45,133,483,500	24.0%	722,135,736	10,832,036,040	2,286,763,164
20	7 Bil or more	0	0	0	25.0%	0	0	0
Total		100,000,000		20,369,323,343,867			434,296,527,046	
							paid into U.S. Treasury	

Amortization Plan C, year 7

NET WORTH TAX TABLE for 2000 (payable by 4/15/01)

Plan C - Based on 50% of maximum proposed amortization rate

Note: These data are projected from the same sources as shown on Distribution of Wealth Graph, p. 36, and Appendix II, and do not indicate household yearly increases or decreases except for Net Worth Taxes paid. Tables for subsequent years follow on sequential pages. All tables are summarized page 51-53.

Bracket	Household Net Worth dollars	Number of Households	end 2000 per Household av Net Worth dollars	end 2000 Bracket Group Net Worth dollars	NW Tax yearly percent	Pay by 4/15/01 Net Worth Tax Av Household dollars	Pay by 4/15/01 Bracket Group Net Worth Tax dollars	After 4/15/01 per Household av Net Worth dollars	Bracket
0	under 150K	80,000,000	100,000	8,000,000,000,000	0.0%	0	0	100,000	0
1	150-200K	10,000,000	169,815	1,698,151,891,373	0.5%	849	8,490,759,457	168,966	1
2	200-600K	5,000,000	376,592	1,882,960,298,802	1.0%	3,766	18,829,602,988	372,826	2
3	600-800K	3,000,000	639,316	1,917,947,335,143	1.5%	9,590	28,769,210,027	629,726	3
4	800K-1.5M	1,000,000	1,063,011	1,063,010,857,037	2.0%	21,260	21,260,217,141	1,041,751	4
5	1.5-4M	800,000	3,053,948	2,443,158,528,671	2.5%	76,349	61,078,963,217	2,977,599	5
6	4-5M	140,000	4,581,528	641,413,916,110	3.0%	137,446	19,242,417,483	4,444,082	6
7	5-6.5M	0	0	0	4.0%	0	0	0	7
8	6.5-15M	25,000	9,076,915	226,922,866,636	5.0%	453,846	11,346,143,332	8,623,069	8
9	15-35M	22,000	28,029,306	616,644,736,051	6.0%	1,681,758	36,998,684,163	26,347,548	9
10	35-65M	0	0	0	8.0%	0	0	0	10
11	65-135M	11,000	88,948,805	978,436,854,410	10.0%	8,894,880	97,843,685,441	80,053,924	11
12	135-185M	1,300	136,690,202	177,697,262,181	15.0%	20,503,530	26,654,589,327	116,186,671	12
13	185-260M	320	209,127,309	66,920,738,734	16.0%	33,460,369	10,707,318,197	175,666,939	13
14	260-400M	180	302,183,114	54,392,960,526	17.5%	52,882,045	9,518,768,092	249,301,069	14
15	400-500M	0	0	0	19.0%	0	0	0	15
16	500-900M	125	566,710,194	70,838,774,195	20.0%	113,342,039	14,167,754,839	453,368,155	16
17	900-1.2B	0	0	0	21.5%	0	0	0	17
18	1.2B-3.0B	75	1,774,168,262	133,062,619,635	22.5%	399,187,859	29,939,089,418	1,374,980,403	18
19	3.0-7B	0	0	0	24.0%	0	0	0	19
20	7 Bil or more	0	0	0	25.0%	0	0	0	20
Total		100,000,000		19,971,559,639,505			394,847,203,122		Total
							paid into U.S. Treasury		

Amortization Plan C, year 8

NET WORTH TAX TABLE for 2001 (payable by 4/15/02)

Plan C - Based on 50% of maximum proposed amortization rate

These data are projected from the same sources as shown on Distribution of Wealth Graph, p. 36, and Appendix II, and do not indicate household yearly increases or decreases except for Net Worth Taxes paid. Tables for subsequent years follow on sequential pages. All tables are summarized page 51-53.

Note:

Household Net Worth dollars	Number of Households	end 2001 per Household av Net Worth dollars	end 2001 Bracket Group Net Worth dollars	NW Tax yearly percent	Pay by 4/15/02 Net Worth Tax Av Household dollars	Pay by 4/15/02 Bracket Group Net Worth Tax dollars	After 4/15/02 per Household av Net Worth dollars	Bracket
under 150K	80,000,000	100,000	8,000,000,000,000	0.0%	0	0	100,000	0
150-200K	10,000,000	168,966	1,689,661,131,917	0.5%	845	8,448,305,660	168,121	1
200-600K	5,000,000	372,826	1,864,130,695,814	1.0%	3,728	18,641,306,958	369,098	2
600-800K	3,000,000	629,726	1,889,178,125,116	1.5%	9,446	28,337,671,877	620,280	3
800K-1.5M	1,000,000	1,041,751	1,041,750,639,896	2.0%	20,835	20,835,012,798	1,020,916	4
1.5-4M	800,000	2,977,599	2,382,079,565,454	2.5%	74,440	59,551,989,136	2,903,159	5
4-5M	140,000	4,444,082	622,171,498,627	3.0%	133,322	18,665,144,959	4,310,760	6
5-6.5M	0	0	0	4.0%	0	0	0	7
6.5-15M	25,000	8,623,069	215,576,723,304	5.0%	431,153	10,778,836,165	8,191,915	8
15-35M	22,000	26,347,548	579,646,051,888	6.0%	1,580,853	34,778,763,113	24,766,695	9
35-65M	0	0	0	8.0%	0	0	0	10
65-135M	12,300	98,120,298	1,206,879,664,648	10.0%	9,812,030	120,687,966,465	88,308,268	11
135-185M	320	175,666,939	56,213,420,537	15.0%	26,350,041	8,432,013,080	149,316,898	12
185-260M	180	249,301,069	44,874,192,434	16.0%	39,888,171	7,179,870,789	209,412,898	13
260-400M	0	0	0	17.5%	0	0	0	14
400-500M	125	453,368,155	56,671,019,356	19.0%	86,139,949	10,767,493,678	367,228,205	15
500-900M	0	0	0	20.0%	0	0	0	16
900-1.2B	0	0	0	21.5%	0	0	0	17
1.2B-3.0B	75	1,374,980,403	103,123,530,217	22.5%	309,370,591	23,202,794,299	1,065,609,812	18
3.0-7B	0	0	0	24.0%	0	0	0	19
7 Bil or more	0	0	0	25.0%	0	0	0	20
	100,000,000		19,751,956,259,208			370,307,168,977		Total
						paid into U.S. Treasury		

Amortization Plan C, year 9

NET WORTH TAX TABLE for 2002 (payable by 4/15/03)

Plan C - Based on 50% of maximum proposed amortization rate

These data are projected from the same sources as shown on Distribution of Wealth Graph, p. 36, and Appendix II, and do not indicate household yearly increases or decreases except for Net Worth Taxes paid. Tables for subsequent years follow on sequential pages. All tables are summarized page 51-53.

Note:

Household Net Worth dollars	Number of Households	end 2002 per Household av Net Worth dollars	end 2002 Bracket Group Net Worth dollars	NW Tax yearly percent	Pay by 4/15/03 Net Worth Tax Av Household dollars	Pay by 4/15/03 Bracket Group Net Worth Tax dollars	After 4/15/03 per Household av Net Worth dollars	Bracket
under 150K	80,000,000	100,000	8,000,000,000,000	0.0%	0	0	100,000	0
150-200K	10,000,000	168,121	1,681,212,826,257	0.5%	841	8,406,064,131	167,281	1
200-600K	5,000,000	369,098	1,845,489,388,856	1.0%	3,691	18,454,893,889	365,407	2
600-800K	3,000,000	620,280	1,860,840,453,239	1.5%	9,304	27,912,606,799	610,976	3
800K-1.5M	1,000,000	1,020,916	1,020,915,627,098	2.0%	20,418	20,418,312,542	1,000,497	4
1.5-4M	800,000	2,903,159	2,322,527,576,318	2.5%	72,579	58,063,189,408	2,830,580	5
4-5M	140,000	4,310,760	603,506,353,668	3.0%	129,323	18,105,190,610	4,181,437	6
5-6.5M	0	0	0	4.0%	0	0	0	7
6.5-15M	25,000	8,191,915	204,797,887,139	5.0%	409,596	10,239,894,357	7,782,320	8
15-35M	22,000	24,766,695	544,867,288,774	6.0%	1,486,002	32,692,037,326	23,280,693	9
35-65M	0	0	0	8.0%	0	0	0	10
65-135M	12,300	88,308,268	1,086,191,698,183	10.0%	8,830,827	108,619,169,818	79,477,441	11
135-185M	320	149,316,898	47,781,407,456	15.0%	22,397,535	7,167,211,118	126,919,364	12
185-260M	180	209,412,898	37,694,321,644	16.0%	33,506,064	6,031,091,463	175,906,834	13
260-400M	125	367,228,205	45,903,525,678	17.5%	64,264,936	8,033,116,994	302,963,269	14
400-500M	0	0	0	19.0%	0	0	0	15
500-900M	0	0	0	20.0%	0	0	0	16
900-1.2B	75	1,065,609,812	79,920,735,918	21.5%	229,106,110	17,182,958,222	836,503,703	17
1.2B-3.0B	0	0	0	22.5%	0	0	0	18
3.0-7B	0	0	0	24.0%	0	0	0	19
7 Bil or more	0	0	0	25.0%	0	0	0	20
	100,000,000		19,381,649,090,231			341,325,736,678		Total
						paid into U.S. Treasury		

Amortization Plan C, year 10

NET WORTH TAX TABLE for 2003 (payable by 4/15/04)

Plan C - Based on 50% of maximum proposed amortization rate

These data are projected from the same sources as shown on Distribution of Wealth Graph, p. 36, and Appendix II, and do not indicate household yearly increases or decreases except for Net Worth Taxes paid. Tables for subsequent years follow on sequential pages. All tables are summarized page 51-53.

Note:

Household Net Worth dollars	Number of Households	end 2003 per Household av Net Worth dollars	end 2003 Bracket Group Net Worth dollars	NW Tax yearly percent	Pay by 4/15/04 Net Worth Tax Av Household dollars	Pay by 4/15/04 Bracket Group Net Worth Tax dollars	After 4/15/04 per Household av Net Worth dollars	Bracket
under 150K	80,000,000	100,000	8,000,000,000,000	0.0%	0	0	100,000	0
150-200K	10,000,000	167,281	1,672,806,762,126	0.5%	836	8,364,033,811	166,444	1
200-600K	5,000,000	365,407	1,827,034,494,967	1.0%	3,654	18,270,344,950	361,753	2
600-800K	3,000,000	610,976	1,832,927,846,441	1.5%	9,165	27,493,917,697	601,811	3
800K-1.5M	1,000,000	1,000,497	1,000,497,314,556	2.0%	20,010	20,009,946,291	980,487	4
1.5-4M	800,000	2,830,580	2,264,464,386,910	2.5%	70,765	56,611,609,673	2,759,816	5
4-5M	140,000	4,181,437	585,401,163,058	3.0%	125,443	17,562,034,892	4,055,994	6
5-6.5M	0	0	0	4.0%	0	0	0	7
6.5-15M	25,000	7,782,320	194,557,992,782	5.0%	389,116	9,727,899,639	7,393,204	8
15-35M	22,000	23,280,693	512,175,251,448	6.0%	1,396,842	30,730,515,087	21,883,852	9
35-65M	0	0	0	8.0%	0	0	0	10
65-135M	12,620	103,198,402	1,302,363,838,830	10.0%	10,319,840	130,236,383,883	92,878,562	11
135-185M	180	175,906,834	31,663,230,181	15.0%	26,386,025	4,749,484,527	149,520,809	12
185-260M	0	0	0	16.0%	0	0	0	13
260-400M	125	302,963,269	37,870,408,685	17.5%	53,018,572	6,627,321,520	249,944,697	14
400-500M	0	0	0	19.0%	0	0	0	15
500-900M	75	836,503,703	62,737,777,696	20.0%	167,300,741	12,547,555,539	669,202,962	16
900-1.2B	0	0	0	21.5%	0	0	0	17
1.2B-3.0B	0	0	0	22.5%	0	0	0	18
3.0-7B	0	0	0	24.0%	0	0	0	19
7 Bil or more	0	0	0	25.0%	0	0	0	20
	100,000,000		19,324,500,467,680			342,931,047,508		Total
						paid into U.S. Treasury		

Amortization Plan C, year 11

NET WORTH TAX TABLE for 2004 (payable by 4/15/05)

Plan C - Based on 50% of maximum proposed amortization rate

These data are projected from the same sources as shown on Distribution of Wealth Graph, p. 36, and Appendix II, and do not indicate household yearly increases or decreases except for Net Worth Taxes paid. Tables for subsequent years follow on sequential pages. All tables are summarized page 51-53.

Note:

Household Net Worth dollars	Number of Households	end 2004 per Household av Net Worth dollars	end 2004 Bracket Group Net Worth dollars	NW Tax yearly percent	Pay by 4/15/05 Net Worth Tax Av Household dollars	Pay by 4/15/05 Bracket Group Net Worth Tax dollars	After 4/15/05 per Household av Net Worth dollars	Bracket
under 150K	80,000,000	100,000	8,000,000,000,000	0.0%	0	0	100,000	0
150-200K	10,000,000	166,444	1,664,442,728,315	0.5%	832	8,322,213,642	165,612	1
200-600K	5,000,000	361,753	1,808,764,150,018	1.0%	3,618	18,087,641,500	358,135	2
600-800K	3,000,000	601,811	1,805,433,928,744	1.5%	9,027	27,081,508,931	592,784	3
800K-1.5M	1,000,000	980,487	980,487,368,265	2.0%	19,610	19,609,747,365	960,878	4
1.5-4M	800,000	2,759,816	2,207,852,777,237	2.5%	68,995	55,196,319,431	2,690,821	5
4-5M	140,000	4,055,994	567,839,128,166	3.0%	121,680	17,035,173,845	3,934,314	6
5-6.5M	0	0	0	4.0%	0	0	0	7
6.5-15M	25,000	7,393,204	184,830,093,143	5.0%	369,660	9,241,504,657	7,023,544	8
15-35M	22,000	21,883,852	481,444,736,361	6.0%	1,313,031	28,886,684,182	20,570,821	9
35-65M	0	0	0	8.0%	0	0	0	10
65-135M	12,620	92,878,562	1,172,127,454,947	10.0%	9,287,856	117,212,745,495	83,590,706	11
135-185M	180	149,520,809	26,913,745,654	15.0%	22,428,121	4,037,061,848	127,092,688	12
185-260M	125	249,944,697	31,243,087,165	16.0%	39,991,152	4,998,893,946	209,953,546	13
260-400M	0	0	0	17.5%	0	0	0	14
400-500M	0	0	0	19.0%	0	0	0	15
500-900M	75	669,202,962	50,190,222,157	20.0%	133,840,592	10,038,044,431	535,362,370	16
900-1.2B	0	0	0	21.5%	0	0	0	17
1.2B-3.0B	0	0	0	22.5%	0	0	0	18
3.0-7B	0	0	0	24.0%	0	0	0	19
7 Bil or more	0	0	0	25.0%	0	0	0	20
	100,000,000		18,981,569,420,172			319,747,539,273		Total
						paid into U.S. Treasury		

Amortization Plan C, year 12

NET WORTH TAX TABLE for 2005 (payable by 4/15/06)

Plan C - Based on 50% of maximum proposed amortization rate

These data are projected from the same sources as shown on Distribution of Wealth Graph, p. 36, and Appendix II, and do not indicate household yearly increases or decreases except for Net Worth Taxes paid.

Tables for subsequent years follow on sequential pages. All tables are summarized page 51-53.

Note:

Household Net Worth dollars	Number of Households	end 2005 per Household av Net Worth dollars	end 2005 Bracket Group Net Worth dollars	NW Tax yearly percent	Pay by 4/15/06 Net Worth Tax Av Household dollars	Pay by 4/15/06 Bracket Group Net Worth Tax dollars	After 4/15/06 per Household av Net Worth dollars	Bracket
under 150K	80,000,000	100,000	8,000,000,000,000	0.0%	0	0	100,000	0
150-200K	10,000,000	165,612	1,656,120,514,674	0.5%	828	8,280,602,573	164,784	1
200-600K	8,000,000	475,460	3,803,677,766,565	1.0%	4,755	38,036,777,666	470,705	2
600-800K	0	0	0	1.5%	0	0	0	3
800K-1.5M	1,000,000	960,878	960,877,620,900	2.0%	19,218	19,217,552,418	941,660	4
1.5-4M	940,000	3,312,567	3,113,813,229,898	2.5%	82,814	77,845,330,747	3,229,753	5
4-5M	0	0	0	3.0%	0	0	0	6
5-6.5M	0	0	0	4.0%	0	0	0	7
6.5-15M	25,000	7,023,544	175,588,588,486	5.0%	351,177	8,779,429,424	6,672,366	8
15-35M	22,000	20,570,821	452,558,052,179	6.0%	1,234,249	27,153,483,131	19,336,571	9
35-65M	0	0	0	8.0%	0	0	0	10
65-135M	12,800	105,341,697	1,348,373,720,256	10.0%	10,534,170	134,837,372,026	94,807,527	11
135-185M	0	0	0	15.0%	0	0	0	12
185-260M	125	209,953,546	26,244,193,218	16.0%	33,592,567	4,199,070,915	176,360,978	13
260-400M	0	0	0	17.5%	0	0	0	14
400-500M	0	0	0	19.0%	0	0	0	15
500-900M	75	535,362,370	40,152,177,725	20.0%	107,072,474	8,030,435,545	428,289,896	16
900-1.2B	0	0	0	21.5%	0	0	0	17
1.2B-3.0B	0	0	0	22.5%	0	0	0	18
3.0-7B	0	0	0	24.0%	0	0	0	19
7 Bil or more	0	0	0	25.0%	0	0	0	20
	100,000,000		19,577,405,863,900			326,380,054,445		Total
						paid into U.S. Treasury		

Amortization Plan C, year 13

NET WORTH TAX TABLE for 2006 (payable by 4/15/07)

Plan C - Based on 50% of maximum proposed amortization rate

These data are projected from the same sources as shown on Distribution of Wealth Graph, p. 36, and Appendix II, and do not indicate household yearly increases or decreases except for Net Worth Taxes paid. Tables for subsequent years follow on sequential pages. All tables are summarized page 51-53.

Note:

Household Net Worth dollars	Number of Households	end 2006 per Household av Net Worth dollars	end 2006 Bracket Group Net Worth dollars	NW Tax yearly percent	Pay by 4/15/07 Net Worth Tax Av Household dollars	Pay by 4/15/07 Bracket Group Net Worth Tax dollars	After 4/15/07 per Household av Net Worth dollars	Bracket
under 150K	80,000,000	100,000	8,000,000,000,000	0.0%	0	0	100,000	0
150-200K	10,000,000	164,784	1,647,839,912,100	0.5%	824	8,239,199,561	163,960	1
200-600K	8,000,000	470,705	3,765,640,988,899	1.0%	4,707	37,656,409,889	465,998	2
600-800K	0	0	0	1.5%	0	0	0	3
800K-1.5M	1,000,000	941,660	941,660,068,482	2.0%	18,833	18,833,201,370	922,827	4
1.5-4M	940,000	3,229,753	3,035,967,899,150	2.5%	80,744	75,899,197,479	3,149,009	5
4-5M	0	0	0	3.0%	0	0	0	6
5-6.5M	0	0	0	4.0%	0	0	0	7
6.5-15M	25,000	6,672,366	166,809,159,061	5.0%	333,618	8,340,457,953	6,338,748	8
15-35M	22,000	19,336,571	425,404,569,049	6.0%	1,160,194	25,524,274,143	18,176,377	9
35-65M	0	0	0	8.0%	0	0	0	10
65-135M	12,800	94,807,527	1,213,536,348,230	10.0%	9,480,753	121,353,634,823	85,326,774	11
135-185M	125	176,360,978	22,045,122,303	15.0%	26,454,147	3,306,768,346	149,906,832	12
185-260M	0	0	0	16.0%	0	0	0	13
260-400M	0	0	0	17.5%	0	0	0	14
400-500M	75	428,289,896	32,121,742,180	19.0%	81,375,080	6,103,131,014	346,914,816	15
500-900M	0	0	0	20.0%	0	0	0	16
900-1.2B	0	0	0	21.5%	0	0	0	17
1.2B-3.0B	0	0	0	22.5%	0	0	0	18
3.0-7B	0	0	0	24.0%	0	0	0	19
7 Bil or more	0	0	0	25.0%	0	0	0	20
	100,000,000		19,251,025,809,455			305,256,274,577		Total
						paid into U.S. Treasury		

Amortization Plan C, year 14

NET WORTH TAX TABLE for 2007 (payable by 4/15/08)

Plan C - Based on 50% of maximum proposed amortization rate

These data are projected from the same sources as shown on Distribution of Wealth Graph, p. 36, and Appendix II, and do not indicate household yearly increases or decreases except for Net Worth Taxes paid. Tables for subsequent years follow on sequential pages. All tables are summarized page 51-53.

Note:

Household Net Worth dollars	Number of Households	end 2007 per Household av Net Worth dollars	end 2007 Bracket Group Net Worth dollars	NW Tax yearly percent	Pay by 4/15/08 Net Worth Tax Av Household dollars	Pay by 4/15/08 Bracket Group Net Worth Tax dollars	After 4/15/08 per Household av Net Worth dollars	Bracket
under 150K	80,000,000	100,000	8,000,000,000,000	0.0%	0	0	100,000	0
150-200K	10,000,000	163,960	1,639,600,712,540	0.5%	820	8,198,003,563	163,140	1
200-600K	8,000,000	465,998	3,727,984,579,010	1.0%	4,660	37,279,845,790	461,338	2
600-800K	0	0	0	1.5%	0	0	0	3
800K-1.5M	1,000,000	922,827	922,826,867,112	2.0%	18,457	18,456,537,342	904,370	4
1.5-4M	940,000	3,149,009	2,960,068,701,671	2.5%	78,725	74,001,717,542	3,070,284	5
4-5M	0	0	0	3.0%	0	0	0	6
5-6.5M	25,000	6,338,748	158,468,701,108	4.0%	253,550	6,338,748,044	6,085,198	7
6.5-15M	0	0	0	5.0%	0	0	0	8
15-35M	22,000	18,176,377	399,880,294,906	6.0%	1,090,583	23,992,817,694	17,085,794	9
35-65M	0	0	0	8.0%	0	0	0	10
65-135M	12,800	85,326,774	1,092,182,713,407	10.0%	8,532,677	109,218,271,341	76,794,097	11
135-185M	125	149,906,832	18,738,353,958	15.0%	22,486,025	2,810,753,094	127,420,807	12
185-260M	0	0	0	16.0%	0	0	0	13
260-400M	75	346,914,816	26,018,611,166	17.5%	60,710,093	4,553,256,954	286,204,723	14
400-500M	0	0	0	19.0%	0	0	0	15
500-900M	0	0	0	20.0%	0	0	0	16
900-1.2B	0	0	0	21.5%	0	0	0	17
1.2B-3.0B	0	0	0	22.5%	0	0	0	18
3.0-7B	0	0	0	24.0%	0	0	0	19
7 Bil or more	0	0	0	25.0%	0	0	0	20
	100,000,000		18,945,769,534,879			284,849,951,364		Total
						paid into U.S. Treasury		

Amortization Plan C, year 15

NET WORTH TAX TABLE for 2008 (payable by 4/15/09)

Plan C - Based on 50% of maximum proposed amortization rate

These data are projected from the same sources as shown on Distribution of Wealth Graph, p. 36, and Appendix II, and do not indicate household yearly increases or decreases except for Net Worth Taxes paid. Tables for subsequent years follow on sequential pages. All tables are summarized page 51-53.

Note:

Household Net Worth dollars	Number of Households	end 2008 per Household av Net Worth dollars	end 2008 Bracket Group Net Worth dollars	NW Tax yearly percent	Pay by 4/15/09 Net Worth Tax Av Household dollars	Pay by 4/15/09 Bracket Group Net Worth Tax dollars	After 4/15/09 per Household av Net Worth dollars	Bracket
under 150K	80,000,000	100,000	8,000,000,000,000	0.0%	0	0	100,000	0
150-200K	10,000,000	163,140	1,631,402,708,977	0.5%	816	8,157,013,545	162,325	1
200-600K	8,000,000	461,338	3,690,704,733,220	1.0%	4,613	36,907,047,332	456,725	2
600-800K	0	0	0	1.5%	0	0	0	3
800K-1.5M	1,000,000	904,370	904,370,329,770	2.0%	18,087	18,087,406,595	886,283	4
1.5-4M	940,000	3,070,284	2,886,066,984,130	2.5%	76,757	72,151,674,603	2,993,527	5
4-5M	0	0	0	3.0%	0	0	0	6
5-6.5M	25,000	6,085,198	152,129,953,064	4.0%	243,408	6,085,198,123	5,841,790	7
6.5-15M	0	0	0	5.0%	0	0	0	8
15-35M	22,000	17,085,794	375,887,477,211	6.0%	1,025,148	22,553,248,633	16,060,647	9
35-65M	0	0	0	8.0%	0	0	0	10
65-135M	12,925	102,107,452	1,319,738,816,779	10.0%	10,210,745	131,973,881,678	91,896,707	11
135-185M	0	0	0	15.0%	0	0	0	12
185-260M	0	0	0	16.0%	0	0	0	13
260-400M	75	286,204,723	21,465,354,212	17.5%	50,085,826	3,756,436,987	236,118,896	14
400-500M	0	0	0	19.0%	0	0	0	15
500-900M	0	0	0	20.0%	0	0	0	16
900-1.2B	0	0	0	21.5%	0	0	0	17
1.2B-3.0B	0	0	0	22.5%	0	0	0	18
3.0-7B	0	0	0	24.0%	0	0	0	19
7 Bil or more	0	0	0	25.0%	0	0	0	20
	100,000,000		18,981,766,357,363			299,671,907,496		Total
						paid into U.S. Treasury		

Amortization Plan C, year 16

NET WORTH TAX TABLE for 2009 (payable by 4/15/10)

Plan C - Based on 50% of maximum proposed amortization rate

These data are projected from the same sources as shown on Distribution of Wealth Graph, p. 36, and Appendix II, and do not indicate household yearly increases or decreases except for Net Worth Taxes paid.

Tables for subsequent years follow on sequential pages. All tables are summarized page 51-53.

Note:

Household Net Worth dollars	Number of Households	end 2010 per Household av Net Worth dollars	end 2010 Bracket Group Net Worth dollars	NW Tax yearly percent	Pay by 4/15/11 Net Worth Tax Av Household dollars	Pay by 4/15/11 Bracket Group Net Worth Tax dollars	After 4/15/11 per Household av Net Worth dollars	Bracket
under 150K	80,000,000	100,000	8,000,000,000,000	0.0%	0	0	100,000	0
150-200K	10,000,000	162,325	1,623,245,695,432	0.5%	812	8,116,228,477	161,513	1
200-600K	8,000,000	456,725	3,653,797,685,888	1.0%	4,567	36,537,976,859	452,157	2
600-800K	0	0	0	1.5%	0	0	0	3
800K-1.5M	1,000,000	886,283	886,282,923,174	2.0%	17,726	17,725,658,463	868,557	4
1.5-4M	940,000	2,993,527	2,813,915,309,526	2.5%	74,838	70,347,882,738	2,918,689	5
4-5M	0	0	0	3.0%	0	0	0	6
5-6.5M	25,000	5,841,790	146,044,754,941	4.0%	233,672	5,841,790,198	5,608,119	7
6.5-15M	0	0	0	5.0%	0	0	0	8
15-35M	22,000	16,060,647	353,334,228,579	6.0%	963,639	21,200,053,715	15,097,008	9
35-65M	0	0	0	8.0%	0	0	0	10
65-135M	12,925	91,896,707	1,187,764,935,101	10.0%	9,189,671	118,776,493,510	82,707,036	11
135-185M	0	0	0	15.0%	0	0	0	12
185-260M	75	236,118,896	17,708,917,225	16.0%	37,779,023	2,833,426,756	198,339,873	13
260-400M	0	0	0	17.5%	0	0	0	14
400-500M	0	0	0	19.0%	0	0	0	15
500-900M	0	0	0	20.0%	0	0	0	16
900-1.2B	0	0	0	21.5%	0	0	0	17
1.2B-3.0B	0	0	0	22.5%	0	0	0	18
3.0-7B	0	0	0	24.0%	0	0	0	19
7 Bil or more	0	0	0	25.0%	0	0	0	20
	100,000,000		18,682,094,449,867			281,379,510,716		Total
						paid into U.S. Treasury		

Amortization Plan C, year 17

NET WORTH TAX TABLE for 2010 (payable by 4/15/11)

Plan C - Based on 50% of maximum proposed amortization rate

These data are projected from the same sources as shown on Distribution of Wealth Graph, p. 36, and Appendix II, and do not indicate household yearly increases or decreases except for Net Worth Taxes paid.

Tables for subsequent years follow on sequential pages. All tables are summarized page 51-53.

Note:

Household Net Worth dollars	Number of Households	end 2011 per Household av Net Worth dollars	end 2011 Bracket Group Net Worth dollars	NW Tax yearly percent	Pay by 4/15/12 Net Worth Tax Av Household dollars	Pay by 4/15/12 Bracket Group Net Worth Tax dollars	After 4/15/12 per Household av Net Worth dollars	Bracket
under 150K	80,000,000	100,000	8,000,000,000,000	0.0%	0	0	100,000	0
150-200K	10,000,000	161,513	1,615,129,466,955	0.5%	808	8,075,647,335	160,705	1
200-600K	8,000,000	452,157	3,617,259,709,029	1.0%	4,522	36,172,597,090	447,636	2
600-800K	0	0	0	1.5%	0	0	0	3
800K-1.5M	1,000,000	868,557	868,557,264,711	2.0%	17,371	17,371,145,294	851,186	4
1.5-4M	940,000	2,918,689	2,743,567,426,788	2.5%	72,967	68,589,185,670	2,845,722	5
4-5M	0	0	0	3.0%	0	0	0	6
5-6.5M	25,000	5,608,119	140,202,964,744	4.0%	224,325	5,608,118,590	5,383,794	7
6.5-15M	0	0	0	5.0%	0	0	0	8
15-35M	22,000	15,097,008	332,134,174,864	6.0%	905,820	19,928,050,492	14,191,187	9
35-65M	0	0	0	8.0%	0	0	0	10
65-135M	12,925	82,707,036	1,068,988,441,591	10.0%	8,270,704	106,898,844,159	74,436,332	11
135-185M	0	0	0	15.0%	0	0	0	12
185-260M	75	198,339,873	14,875,490,469	16.0%	31,734,380	2,380,078,475	166,605,493	13
260-400M	0	0	0	17.5%	0	0	0	14
400-500M	0	0	0	19.0%	0	0	0	15
500-900M	0	0	0	20.0%	0	0	0	16
900-1.2B	0	0	0	21.5%	0	0	0	17
1.2B-3.0B	0	0	0	22.5%	0	0	0	18
3.0-7B	0	0	0	24.0%	0	0	0	19
7 Bil or more	0	0	0	25.0%	0	0	0	20
	100,000,000		18,400,714,939,151			265,023,667,105		Total
						paid into U.S. Treasury		

Amortization Plan C, year 18

NET WORTH TAX TABLE for 2011 (payable by 4/15/12)

Plan C - Based on 50% of maximum proposed amortization rate

These data are projected from the same sources as shown on Distribution of Wealth Graph, p. 36, and Appendix II, and do not indicate household yearly increases or decreases except for Net Worth Taxes paid.

Tables for subsequent years follow on sequential pages. All tables are summarized page 51-53.

Household Net Worth dollars	Number of Households	end 2012 per Household av Net Worth dollars	end 2012 Bracket Group Net Worth dollars	NW Tax yearly percent	Pay by 4/15/13 Net Worth Tax Av Household dollars	Pay by 4/15/13 Bracket Group Net Worth Tax dollars	After 4/15/13 per Household av Net Worth dollars
under 150K	80,000,000	100,000	8,000,000,000,000	0.0%	0	0	100,000
150-200K	10,000,000	160,705	1,607,053,819,620	0.5%	804	8,035,269,098	159,902
200-600K	8,000,000	447,636	3,581,087,111,939	1.0%	4,476	35,810,871,119	443,160
600-800K	0	0	0	1.5%	0	0	0
800K-1.5M	1,000,000	851,186	851,186,119,417	2.0%	17,024	17,023,722,388	834,162
1.5-4M	940,000	2,845,722	2,674,978,241,119	2.5%	71,143	66,874,456,028	2,774,578
4-5M	0	0	0	3.0%	0	0	0
5-6.5M	25,000	5,383,794	134,594,846,154	4.0%	215,352	5,383,793,846	5,168,442
6.5-15M	22,000	14,191,187	312,206,124,372	5.0%	709,559	15,610,306,219	13,481,628
15-35M	0	0	0	6.0%	0	0	0
35-65M	0	0	0	8.0%	0	0	0
65-135M	12,925	74,436,332	962,089,597,432	10.0%	7,443,633	96,208,959,743	66,992,699
135-185M	75	166,605,493	12,495,411,994	15.0%	24,990,824	1,874,311,799	141,614,669
185-260M	0	0	0	16.0%	0	0	0
260-400M	0	0	0	17.5%	0	0	0
400-500M	0	0	0	19.0%	0	0	0
500-900M	0	0	0	20.0%	0	0	0
900-1.2B	0	0	0	21.5%	0	0	0
1.2B-3.0B	0	0	0	22.5%	0	0	0
3.0-7B	0	0	0	24.0%	0	0	0
7 Bil or more	0	0	0	25.0%	0	0	0
	100,000,000		18,135,691,272,046			246,821,690,241	
						paid into U.S. Treasury	

APPENDIX V
ITEMS TO BE DECLARED FOR NET WORTH TAX

The following items would be declared (list is based on *Balance Sheets of the U.S. Economy, 1945-92, **C.9** Table B.11,* of Federal Reserve Bank, 9/17/93).
All holdings to include both in the United States and abroad. All holdings are taxed at present market values, and are net of any mortgages or loans outstanding:

Real Estate

Common and preferred stock

U.S. Government securities

Tax exempt securities

Mutual fund shares

Equities and deposits in Hedge Funds

Corporate and foreign bonds

Deposits of all items of value

Credits

Credit market instruments

Security market credits

Mortgages

Open market paper

Accounts receivable

Insurance receivables

Tax receivables

Inventories

Stock in trade

Consumer durables

Shares in cooperatives

All life insurances at present values

Life insurance reserves

Pension fund reserves

The principal amounts of all trust accounts and beneficial accounts

Present-value accumulations in all:
Individual Retirement Accounts (IRA's)
Employee Retirement Accounts (ERA's)
Employees Stock Options Plans (ESOP's)
KEOGH Accounts, 401(k) plans, etc.

Additionally:
Personalty: including airplanes, boats, automobiles, jewels, precious metals, show animals, art objects, libraries, antiques, etc., at present market values.

Intangibles such as patents, copyrights, etc., at present market values.

APPENDIX VI

CONGRESSIONAL DIRECTORY FOR POLITICAL ACTION IN 1994

Telephone numbers and Washington, D.C. mailing addresses of all U.S. Senators and Representatives

SENATORS

ALABAMA

Howell Heflin (D)
728 Hart Senate Office Building
Washington, DC 20510
Tel: (202) 224-4124

Richard C. Shelby (D)
509 Hart Senate Office Building
Washington, DC 20510
Tel: (202) 224-5744

ALASKA

Ted Stevens (R)
522 Hart Senate Office Building
Washington, DC 20510
Tel: (202(224-3004

Frank H. Murkowski (R)
706 Hart Senate Office Building
Washington, DC 20510
Tel: (202) 224-6665

ARIZONA

Dennis DeConcini (D)
328 Hart Senate Office Building
Washington, DC 20510
Tel: (202) 224-4521

John McCain (R)
111 Russell Senate Office Building
Washington, DC 20510
Tel: (202) 224-2235

ARKANSAS

Dale Bumpers (D)
229 Dirksen Senate House Building
Washington, DC 20510
Tel: (202) 224-4843

David Pryor (D)
267 Russell Senate Office Building
Washington, DC 20510
Tel: (202) 224-2353

SENATORS (continued)

CALIFORNIA

Dianne Feinstein (D)
331 Hart Senate Office Building
Washington, DC 20510
Tel: (202) 224-3841

Barbara Boxer (D)
112 Hart Senate Office Building
Washington, DC 20510
Tel: (202) 224-3553

COLORADO

Hank Brown (R)
717 Hart Senate Office Building
Washington, DC 20510
Tel: (202) 224-5941

Ben Nighthorse Campbell (D)
380 Russell Senate Office Building
Washington, DC 20510
Tel: (202) 224-5852

CONNECTICUT

Christopher J. Dodd (D)
444 Russell Senate Office Building
Washington, DC 20510
Tel: (202) 224-2823

Joseph I. Lieberman (D)
502 Hart Senate Office Building
Washington, DC 20510
Tel: (202) 224-4041

DELAWARE

William V. Roth (R)
104 Hart Senate Office Building
Washington, DC 20510
Tel: (202) 224-2441

Joseph R. Biden (D)
221 Russell Senate Office Building
Washington, DC 20510
Tel: (202) 224-5042

FLORIDA

Bob Graham (D)
524 Hart Senate Office Building
Washington, D.C. 20510
Tel: (202) 224-3041

Connie Mack (R)
517 Hart Senate Office Building
Washington, D.C. 20510
Tel: (202) 224-5274

GEORGIA

Sam Nunn (D)
303 Dirksen Senate Office Building
Washington, D.C. 20510
Tel: (202) 224-3521

Paul Coverdell (R)
200 Russell Senate Office Building
Washington, D.C. 20510
Tel: (202) 224-3643

HAWAII

Daniel K. Inouye (D)
722 Hart Senate Office Building
Washington, D.C. 20510
Tel: (202) 224-3934

Daniel K. Akaka (D)
720 Hart Senate Office Building
Washington, D.C. 20510
Tel: (202) 224-6361

IDAHO

Larry E. Craig (R)
302 Hart Senate Office Building
Washington, D.C. 20510
Tel: (202) 224-2752

Dirk Kempthorne (R)
367 Dirksen Senate Office Building
Washington, D.C. 20510
Tel: (202) 224-6142

ILLINOIS

Paul Simon (D)
462 Dirksen Senate Office Building
Washington, D.C. 20510
Tel: (202) 224-2152

Carol Moseley-Braun (D)
320 Hart Senate Office Building
Washington, D.C. 20510
Tel: (202) 224-2854

INDIANA

Richard G. Lugar (R)
306 Hart Senate Office Building
Washington, D.C. 20510
Tel: (202) 224-4814

Dan Coats (R)
404 Russell Senate Office Building
Washington, D.C. 20510
Tel: (202) 224-5623

IOWA

Charles E. Grassley (R)
135 Hart Senate Office Building
Washington, D.C. 20510
Tel: (202) 224-3744

Tom Harkin (D)
531 Hart Senate Office Building
Washington, D.C. 20510
Tel: (202) 224-3254

KANSAS

Robert Dole (R)
141 Hart Senate Office Building
Washington, D.C. 20510
Tel: (202) 224-6521

Nancy Landon Kassebaum (R)
302 Russell Senate Office Building
Washington, D.C. 20510
Tel: (202) 224-4774

KENTUCKY

Wendell H. Ford (D)
173A Russell Senate Office Building
Washington, D.C. 20510
Tel: (202) 224-4343

Mitch McConnell (R)
120 Russell Senate Office Building
Washington, D.C. 20510
Tel: (202) 224-2541

LOUISIANA

J. Bennett Johnston (D)
136 Hart Senate Office Building
Washington, D.C. 20510
Tel: (202) 224-5824

John Breaux (D)
516 Hart Senate Office Building
Washington, D.C. 20510
Tel: (202) 224-4623

MAINE

William S. Cohen (R)
322 Hart Senate Office Building
Washington, D.C. 20510
Tel: (202) 224-2523

George J. Mitchell (D)
176 Russell Senate Office Building
Washington, D.C. 20510
Tel: (202) 224-5344

MARYLAND

Paul S. Sarbanes (D)
309 Hart Senate Office Building
Washington, D.C. 20510
Tel: (202) 224-4524

Barbara A. Mikulski (D)
709 Hart Senate Office Building
Washington, D.C. 20510
Tel: (202) 224-44654

MASSACHUSETTS

Edward M. Kennedy (D)
315 Russell Senate Office Building
Washington, D.C. 20510
Tel: (202) 224-4543

John F. Kerry (D)
421 Russell Senate Office Building
Washington, D.C. 20510
Tel: (202) 224-2742

MICHIGAN

Donald W. Riegle, Jr. (D)
105 Dirksen Senate Office Building
Washington, D.C. 20510
Tel: (202) 224-4822

Carl M. Levin (D)
459 Russell Senate Office Building
Washington, D.C. 20510
Tel: (202) 224-6221

MINNESOTA

Dave Durenberger (R)
154 Russell Senate Office Building
Washington, D.C. 20510
Tel: (202) 224-3244

Paul D. Wellstone (D)
702 Hart Senate Office Building
Washington, D.C. 20510
Tel: (202) 224-5641

MISSISSIPPI

Thad Cochran (R)
326 Russell Senate Office Building
Washington, D.C. 20510
Tel: (202) 224-5054

Trent Lott (R)
487 Russell Senate Office Building
Washington, D.C. 20510
Tel: (202) 224-6253

MISSOURI

John C. Danforth (R)
249 Russell Senate Office Building
Washington, D.C. 20510
Tel: (202) 224-6154

Christopher S. Bond (R)
293 Russell Senate Office Building
Washington, D.C. 20510
Tel: (202) 224-5721

MONTANA

Max Baucus (D)
511 Hart Senate Office Building
Washington, D.C. 20510
Tel: (202) 224-2651

Conrad Burns (R)
183 Dirksen Senate Office Building
Washington, D.C. 20510
Tel: (202) 224-2644

NEBRASKA

J. James Exon (D)
528 Hart Senate Office Building
Washington, D.C. 20510
Tel: (202) 224-4224

J. Robert Kerrey (D)
303 Hart Senate Office Building
Washington, D.C. 20510
Tel: (202) 224-6551

NEVADA

Harry Reid (D)
324 Hart Senate Office Building
Washington, D.C. 20510
Tel: (202) 224-3542

Richard H. Bryan (D)
364 Russell Senate Office Building
Washington, D.C. 20510
Tel: (202) 224-6244

NEW HAMPSHIRE

Robert C. Smith (R)
332 Dirksen Senate Office Building
Washington, D.C. 20510
Tel: (202) 224-2841

Judd Gregg (R)
393 Russell Senate Office Building
Washington, D.C. 20510
Tel: (202) 224-3324

NEW JERSEY

Bill Bradley (D)
731 Hart Senate Office Building
Washington, D.C. 20510
Tel: (202) 224-3224

Frank R. Lautenberg (D)
506 Hart Senate Office Building
Washington, D.C. 20510
Tel: (202) 224-4744

NEW MEXICO

Pete V. Domenici (R)
427 Dirksen Senate Office Building
Washington, D.C. 20510
Tel: (202) 224-6621

Jeff Bingaman (D)
110 Hart Senate Office Building
Washington, D.C. 20510
Tel: (202) 224-5521

NEW YORK

Daniel Patrick Moynihan (D)
464 Russell Senate Office Building
Washington, D.C. 20510
Tel: (202) 224-4451

Alfonse M. D'Amato (R)
520 Hart Senate Office Building
Washington, D.C. 20510
Tel: (202) 224-6542

NORTH CAROLINA

Jesse Helms (R)
403 Dirksen Senate Office Building
Washington, D.C. 20510
Tel: (202) 224-6342

Lauch Faircloth (R)
702 Hart Senate Office Building
Washington, D.C. 20510
Tel: (202) 224-3154

NORTH DAKOTA

Kent Conrad (D)
724 Hart Senate Office Building
Washington, D.C. 20510
Tel: (202) 224-2043

Byron L. Dorgan (D)
713 Hart Senate Office Building
Washington, D.C. 20510
Tel: (202) 224-2551

OHIO

John Glenn (D)
503 Hart Senate Office Building
Washington, D.C. 20510
Tel: (202) 224-3353

Howard M. Metzenbaum (D)
140 Russell Senate Office Building
Washington, D.C. 20510
Tel: (202) 224-2315

OKLAHOMA

David L. Boren (D)
453 Russell Senate Office Building
Washington, D.C. 20510
Tel: (202) 224-4721

Don Nickles (R)
713 Hart Senate Office Building
Washington, D.C. 20510
Tel: (202) 224-5754

OREGON

Mark O. Hatfield (R)
711 Hart Senate Office Building
Washington, D.C. 20510
Tel: (202) 224-3753

Bob Packwood (R)
259 Russell Senate Office Building
Washington, D.C. 20510
Tel: (202) 224-5244

PENNSYLVANIA

Arlen Specter (R)
530 Hart Senate Office Building
Washington, D.C. 20510
Tel: (202) 224-4254

Harris Wofford (D)
283 Russell Senate Office Building
Washington, D.C. 20510
Tel: (202) 224-6324

RHODE ISLAND

Claiborne Pell (D)
335 Russell Senate Office Building
Washington, D.C. 20510
Tel: (202) 224-4642

John H. Chafee (R)
567 Dirksen Senate Office Building
Washington, D.C. 20510
Tel: (202) 224-2921

SOUTH CAROLINA

Strom Thurmond (R)
217 Russell Senate Office Building
Washington, D.C. 20510
Tel: (202) 224-5972

Ernest F. Hollings (D)
125 Russell Senate Office Building
Washington, D.C. 20510
Tel: (202) 224-6121

SOUTH DAKOTA

Larry Pressler (R)
133 Hart Senate Office Building
Washington, D.C. 20510
Tel: (202) 224-5842

Thomas A. Daschle (D)
317 Hart Senate Office Building
Washington, D.C. 20510
Tel: (202) 224-2321

TENNESSEE

Jim Sasser (D)
363 Russell Senate Office Building
Washington, D.C. 20510
Tel: (202) 224-3344

Harlan Mathews (D)
506 Dirksen Senate Office Building
Washington, D.C. 20510
Tel: (202) 224-4944

TEXAS

Phil Gramm (R)
370 Russell Senate Office Building
Washington, D.C. 20510
Tel: (202) 224-2934

Kay Bailey Hutchinson (R)
703 Hart Senate Office Building
Washington, D.C. 20510
Tel: (202) 224-5922

UTAH

Orrin G. Hatch (R)
135 Russell Senate Office Building
Washington, D.C. 20510
Tel: (202) 224-5251

Robert F. Bennett (R)
241 Dirksen Senate Office Building
Washington, D.C. 20510
Tel: (202) 224-5444

VERMONT

Patrick J. Leahy (D)
433 Russell Senate Office Building
Washington, D.C. 20510
Tel: (202) 224-4242

James M. Jeffords (R)
530 Dirksen Senate Office Building
Washington, D.C. 20510
Tel: (202) 224-5141

VIRGINIA

John W. Warner (R)
225 Russell Senate Office Building
Washington, D.C. 20510
Tel: (202) 224-2023

Charles S. Robb (D)
493 Russell Senate Office Building
Washington, D.C. 20510
Tel: (202) 224-4024

WASHINGTON

Slade Gorton (R)
730 Hart Senate Office Building
Washington, D.C. 20510
Tel: (202) 224-3441

Patty Murray (D)
302 Hart Senate Office Building
Washington, D.C. 20510
Tel: (202) 224-2621

WEST VIRGINIA

Robert C. Byrd (D)
311 Hart Senate Office Building
Washington, D.C. 20510
Tel: (202) 224-2621

John D. Rockefeller IV (D)
109 Hart Senate Office Building
Washington, D.C. 20510
Tel: (202) 224-6472

WISCONSIN

Herb Kohl (D)
330 Hart Senate Office Building
Washington, D.C. 20510
Tel: (202) 224-5653

Russell Feingold (D)
502 Hart Senate Office Building
Washington, D.C. 20510
Tel: (202) 224-5323

WYOMING

Malcolm Wallop (R)
237 Russell Senate Office Building
Washington, D.C. 20510
Tel: (202) 224-6441

Alan K. Simpson (R)
261 Dirksen Senate Office Building
Washington, D.C. 20510
Tel: (202) 224-3424

MEMBERS OF THE
HOUSE REPRESENTATIVES

ALABAMA

First District
Sonny Callahan (R)
2418 Rayburn House Office Building
Washington, D.C. 20515
Tel: (202) 225-4931

Second District
Terry Everett (R)
208 Cannon House Office Building
Washington, D.C. 20515
Tel: (202) 225-2901

Third District
Glen Browder (D)
1221 Longworth House Office Building
Washington, D.C. 20515
Tel: (202) 225-3261

Fourth District
Tom Bevill (D)
2302 Rayburn House Office Building
Washington, D.C. 20515
Tel: (202) 225-4876

Fifth District
Bud Cramer (D)
1318 Longworth House Office Building
Washington, D.C. 20515
Tel: (202) 225-4801

Sixth District
Spencer Bachus (R)
216 Cannon House Office Building
Washington, D.C. 20515
Tel: (202) 225-4921

Seventh District
Earl F. Hilliard (D)
1007 Longworth House Office Building
Washington, D.C. 20515
Tel: (202) 225-2665

ALASKA

At Large
Don Young (R)
2331 Rayburn House Office Building
Washington, D.C. 20515

ARIZONA

First District
Sam Coppersmith (D)
1607 Longworth House Office Building
Washington, D.C. 20515
Tel: (202) 225-2635

Second District
Ed Pastor (D)
408 Cannon House Office Building
Washington, DC 20515
Tel: (202) 225-4065

Third District
Bob Stump (R)
211 Cannon House Office Building
Washington, DC 20515
Tel: (202) 225-4576

Fourth District
Jon Kyl (R)
2440 Rayburn House Office Building
Washington, DC 20515
Tel: (202) 225-3361

Fifth District
Jim Kolbe (R)
405 Cannon House Office Building
Washington, DC 20515
Tel: (202) 225-2542

Sixth District
Karan English (D)
1024 Longworth House Office Building
Washington, DC 20515
Tel: (202) 225-2150

ARKANSAS

First District
Blanche M. Lambert (D)
1024 Longworth House Office Building
Washington, DC 20515
Tel: (202) 225-4076

Second District
Ray Thornton (D)
1214 Longworth House Office Building
Washington, DC 20515
Tel: (202) 225-2506

Third District
Tim Hutchinson (R)
1541 Longworth House Office Building
Washington, DC 20515
Tel: (202) 225-4301

Fourth District
Jay Dickey (R)
1338 Longworth House Office Building
Washington, DC 20515
Tel: (202) 225-3772

CALIFORNIA

First District
Dan Hamburg (D)
114 Cannon House Office Building
Washington, DC 20515
Tel: (202) 225-3311

Second District
Wally Herger (R)
2433 Rayburn House Office Building
Washington, DC 20515
Tel: (202) 225-3076

Third District
Vic Fazio (D)
2113 Rayburn House Office Building
Washington, DC 20515
Tel: (202) 225-5716

Fourth District
John T. Doolittle (R)
1524 Longworth House Office Building
Washington, DC 20515
Tel: (202) 255-2511

Fifth District
Robert T. Matsui (D)
2311 Rayburn House Office Building
Washington, DC 20515
Tel: (202) 255-7163

Sixth District
Lynn Woolsey (D)
439 Cannon House Office Building
Washington, DC 20515
Tel: (202) 255-5161

CALIFORNIA

Seventh District
George Miller (D)
2205 Rayburn House Office Building
Washington, DC 20515
Tel: (202)225-2095

Eighth District
Nancy Pelosi (D)
240 Cannon House Office Building
Washington, DC 20515
Tel: (202) 225-4965

Ninth District
Ronald V. Dellums (D)
2108 Rayburn House Office Building
Washington, DC 20515
Tel: (202) 225-2661

Tenth District
Bill Baker (R)
1724 Longworth House Office Building
Washington, DC 20515
Tel: (202) 225-1880

Eleventh District
Richard W. Pombo (R)
1519 Longworth House Office Building
Washington, DC 20515
Tel: (202) 225-1947

Twelfth District
Tom Lantos (D)
2182 Rayburn House Office Building
Washington, DC 20515
Tel: (202) 225-3531

Thirteenth District
Fortney Pete Stark (D)
239 Cannon House Office Building
Washington, DC 20515
Tel: (202) 225-5065

Fourteenth District
Anna G. Eshoo (D)
1505 Longworth House Office Building
Washington, DC 20515
Tel: (202) 225-8104

Fifteenth District
Norman Y. Mineta (D)
2221 Rayburn House Office Building
Washington, DC 20515
Tel: (202) 225-2631

Sixteenth District
Don Edwards (D)
2307 Rayburn House Office Building
Washington, DC 20515
Tel: (202) 225-3072

Seventeenth District
Sam Farr (D)
1216 Longworth House Office Building
Washington, DC 20515
Tel: (202) 225-2861

Eighteenth District
Gary A. Condit (D)
1123 Longworth House Office Building
Washington, DC 20515
Tel: (202) 225-6131

Nineteenth District
Richard H. Lehman (D)
1226 Longworth House Office Building
Washington, DC 20515
Tel: (202) 225-4540

Twentieth District
Calvin M. Dooley (D)
1227 Longworth House Office Building
Washington, DC 20515
Tel: (202) 225-3341

Twenty-First District
Bill Thomas (R)
2209 Rayburn House Office Building
Washington, DC 20515
Tel: (202) 225-2915

Twenty-Second District
Michael Huffington (R)
113 Cannon House Office Building
Washington, DC 20515
Tel: (202) 225-3601

Twenty-Third District
Elton Gallegly (R)
2441 Rayburn House Office Building
Washington, DC 20515
Tel: (202) 225-5811

Twenty-Fourth District
Anthony C. Beilenson (D)
2465 Rayburn House Office Building
Washington, DC 20515
Tel: (202) 225-5911

Twenty-Fifth District
Howard P. (Buck) McKeon (R)
307 Cannon House Office Building
Washington, DC 20515
Tel: (202) 225-1956

Twenty-Sixth District
Howard L. Berman (D)
2201 Rayburn House Office Building
Washington, DC 20515
Tel: (202) 225-4695

Twenty-Seventh District
Carlos J. Moorhead (R)
2346 Rayburn House Office Building
Washington, DC 20515
Tel: (202) 225-4176

Twenty-Eighth District
David Dreier (R)
411 Cannon House Office Building
Washington, DC 20515
Tel: (202) 225-2305

Twenty-Ninth District
Henry A. Waxman (D)
2408 Rayburn House Office Building
Washington, DC 20515
Tel: (202) 225-3976

Thirtieth District
Xavier Becerra (D)
1710 Longworth House Office Building
Washington, DC 20515
Tel: (202) 225-6235

Thirty-First District
Matthew G. Martinez, Jr. (D)
2231 Rayburn House Office Building
Washington, DC 20515
Tel: (202) 225-5464

Thirty-Second District
Julian C. Dixon (D)
2400 Rayburn House Office Building
Washington, DC 20515
Tel: (202) 225-7084

Thirty-Third District
Lucille Roybal-Allard (D)
324 Cannon House Office Building
Washington, DC 20515
Tel: (202) 225-1766

Thirty-Fourth District
Esteban Edward Torres (D)
1740 Longworth House Office Building
Washington, DC 20515
Tel: (202) 225-5256

Thirty-Fifth District
Maxine Waters (D)
1207 Longworth House Office Building
Washington, DC 20515
Tel: (202) 225-2201

Thirty-Sixth District
Jane Harman (D)
325 Cannon House Office Building
Washington, DC 20515
Tel: (202) 225-8220

Thirty-Seventh District
Walter R. Tucker III (D)
419 Cannon House Office Building
Washington, DC 20515
Tel: (202) 225-7924

Thirty-Eighth District
Steve Horn (R)
1023 Longworth House Office Building
Washington, DC 20515
Tel: (202) 225-6676

Thirty-Ninth District
Ed Royce (R)
1404 Longworth House Office Building
Washington, DC 20515
Tel: (202) 225-4111

Fortieth District
Jerry Lewis (R)
2312 Rayburn House Office Building
Washington, DC 20515
Tel: (202) 225-5861

Forty-First District
Jay Kim (R)
502 Cannon House Office Building
Washington, DC 20515
Tel: (202) 225-3201

Forty-Second District
George E. Brown, Jr. (D)
2300 Rayburn House Office Building
Washington, DC 20515
Tel: (202) 225-6161

Forty-Third District
Ken Calvert (R)
1523 Longworth House Office Building
Washington, DC 20515
Tel: (202) 225-1986

Forty-Fourth District
Alfred A. (Al) McCandless (R)
2422 Rayburn House Office Building
Washington, DC 20515
Tel: (202) 225-5330

Forty-Fifth District
Dana Rohrabacher (R)
1027 Longworth House Office Building
Washington, DC 20515
Tel: (202) 225-2415

Forty-Sixth District
Robert K. Dornan (R)
2402 Rayburn House Office Building
Washington, DC 20515
Tel: (202) 225-2965

Forty-Seventh District
Christopher Cox (R)
206 Cannon House Office Building
Washington, DC 20515
Tel: (202) 225-5611

Forty-Eighth District
Ron Packard (R)
2162 Rayburn House Office Building
Washington, DC 20515
Tel: (202) 225-3906

Forty-Ninth District
Lynn Schenk (D)
315 Cannon House Office Building
Washington, DC 20515
Tel: (202) 225-2040

Fiftieth District
Bob Filner (D)
504 Cannon House Office Building
Washington, DC 20515
Tel: (202) 225-8045

Fifty-First District
Randy (Duke) Cunningham (R)
117 Cannon House Office Building
Washington, DC 20515
Tel: (202) 225-5452

Fifty-Second District
Duncan Hunter (R)
133 Cannon House Office Building
Washington, DC 20515
Tel: (202) 225-5672

COLORADO

First District
Patricia Schroeder (D)
2208 Rayburn House Office Building
Washington, DC 20515
Tel: (202) 225-4431

Second District
David E. Skaggs (D)
1124 Longworth House Office Building
Washington, DC 20515
Tel: (202) 225-2161

Third District
Scott McInnins (R)
512 Cannon House Office Building
Washington, DC 20515
Tel: (202) 225-4761

Fourth District
Wayne Allard (R)
422 Cannon House Office Building
Washington, DC 20515
Tel: (202) 225-4676

Fifth District
Joel Hefley (R)
2442 Rayburn House Office Building

Washington, DC 20515
Tel: (202) 225-4422

Sixth District
Dan Schaefer (R)
2448 Rayburn House Office Building
Washington, DC 20515
Tel: (202) 225-7882

CONNECTICUT

First District
Barbara B. Kennelly (D)
201 Cannon House Office Building
Washington, DC 20515
Tel: (202) 225-2265

Second District
Sam Gejdenson (D)
2416 Rayburn House Office Building
Washington, DC 20515
Tel: (202) 225-2076

Third District
Rosa L. DeLauro (D)
327 Cannon House Office Building
Washington, DC 20515
Tel: (202) 225-3661

Fourth District
Christopher Shays (R)
1034 Longworth House Office Building
Washington, DC 20515
Tel: (202) 225-5541

Fifth District
Gary A. Franks (R)
435 Cannon House Office Building
Washington, DC 20515
Tel: (202) 225-3822

Sixth District
Nancy L. Johnson (R)
343 Cannon House Office Building
Washington, DC 20515
Tel: (202) 225-4476

DELAWARE

At Large
Michael N. Castle (R)
1205 Longworth House Office Building
Washington, DC 20515
Tel: (202) 225-4165

FLORIDA

First District
Earl Hutto (D)
2435 Rayburn House Office Building
Washington, DC 20515
Tel: (202) 225-4136

Second District
Pete Peterson (D)
426 Cannon House Office Building
Washington, DC 20515
Tel: (202) 225-5235

Third District
Corrine Brown (D)
1037 Longworth House Office Building
Washington, DC 20515
Tel: (202) 225-0123

Fourth District
Tillie Fowler (R)
413 Cannon House Office Building
Washington, DC 20515
Tel: (202) 225-2501

Fifth District
Karen L. Thurman (D)
130 Cannon House Office Building
Washington, DC 20515
Tel: (202) 225-1002

Sixth District
Cliff Stearns (R)
332 Cannon House Office Building
Washington, DC 20515
Tel: (202) 225-5744

Seventh District
John L. Mica (R)
427 Cannon House Office Building
Washington, DC 20515
Tel: (202) 225-4035

Eighth District
Bill McCollum (R)
2266 Rayburn House Office Building
Washington, DC 20515
Tel: (202) 225-2176

Ninth District
Michael Bilirakis (R)
2240 Rayburn House Office Building

Washington, DC 20515
Tel: (202) 225-5755

Tenth District
C.W. Bill Young (R)
2407 Rayburn House Office Building
Washington, DC 20515
Tel: (202) 225-5961

Eleventh District
Sam Gibbons (D)
2204 Rayburn House Office Building
Washington, DC 20515
Tel: (202) 225-3376

Twelfth District
Charles T. Canady (R)
1107 Longworth House Office Building
Washington, DC 20515
Tel: (202) 225-1252

Thirteenth District
Dan Miller (R)
510 Cannon House Office Building
Washington, DC 20515
Tel: (202) 225-5015

Fourteenth District
Porter J. Goss (R)
330 Cannon House Office Building
Washington, DC 20515
Tel: (202) 225-2536

Fifteenth District
Jim Bacchus (D)
432 Cannon House Office Building
Washington, DC 20515
Tel: (202) 225-3671

Sixteenth District
Tom Lewis (R)
2351 Rayburn House Office Building
Washington, DC 20515
Tel: (202) 225-5792

Seventeenth District
Carrie P. Meek (D)
404 Cannon House Office Building
Washington, DC 20515
Tel: (202) 225-4506

Eighteenth District
Ileana Ros-Lehtinen (R)
127 Cannon House Office Building
Washington, DC 20515
Tel: (202) 225-3931

Nineteenth District
Harry A. Johnston (D)
204 Cannon House Office Building
Washington, DC 20515
Tel: (202) 225-3001

Twentieth District
Peter Deutsch (D)
425 Cannon House Office Building
Washington, DC 20515
Tel: (202) 225-7931

Twenty-First District
Lincoln Diaz-Balart (R)
509 Cannon House Office Building
Washington, DC 20515
Tel: (202) 225-4211

Twenty-Second District
E. Clay Shaw, Jr. (R)
2267 Rayburn House Office Building
Washington, DC 20515
Tel: (202) 225-3026

Twenty-Third District
Alcee L. Hastings (D)
1039 Longworth House Office Building
Washington, DC 20515
Tel: (202) 225-1313

GEORGIA

First District
Jack Kingston (R)
1229 Longworth House Office Building
Washington, DC 20515
Tel: (202) 225-5831

Second District
Sanford Bishop (D)
1632 Longworth House Office Building
Washington, DC 20515
Tel: (202) 225-3631

Third District
Mac Collins (R)
1118 Longworth House Office Building
Washington, DC 20515
Tel: (202) 225-5901

Fourth District

John Linder (R)
1605 Longworth House Office Building
Washington, DC 20515
Tel: (202) 225-4272

Fifth District
John Lewis (D)
329 Cannon House Office Building
Washington, DC 20515
Tel: (202) 225-3801

Sixth District
Newt Gingrich (R)
2428 Rayburn House Office Building
Washington, DC 20515
Tel: (202) 225-4501

Seventh District
George (Buddy) Darden (D)
2303 Rayburn House Office Building
Washington, DC 20515
Tel: (202) 225-2931

Eighth District
J. Roy Rowland (D)
2134 Rayburn House Office Building
Washington, DC 20515
Tel: (202) 225-6531

Ninth District
Nathan Deal (D)
1406 Longworth House Office Building
Washington, DC 20515
Tel: (202) 225-5211

Tenth District
Don Johnson (D)
226 Cannon House Office Building
Washington, DC 20515
Tel: (202) 225-4101

Eleventh District
Cynthia McKinney (D)
124 Cannon House Office Building
Washington, DC 20515
Tel: (202) 225-1605

HAWAII

First District
Neil Abercrombie (D)
1440 Longworth House Office Building
Washington, DC 20515
Tel: (202) 225-2726

Second District
Patsy T. Mink (D)
2135 Rayburn House Office Building
Washington, DC 2051
5Tel: (202) 225-4906

IDAHO

First District
Larry LaRocco (D)
1117 Longworth House Office Building
Washington, DC 20515
Tel: (202) 225-6611

Second District
Michael D. Crapo (R)
437 Cannon House Office Building
Washington, DC 20515
Tel: (202) 225-5531

ILLINOIS

First District
Bobby Rush (D)
1725 Longworth House Office Building
Washington, DC 20515
Tel: (202) 225-4372

Second District
Mel Reynolds (D)
514 Cannon House Office Building
Washington, DC 20515
Tel: (202) 225-0773

Third District
William O. Lipinski (D)
1501 Longworth House Office Building
Washington, DC 20515
Tel: (202) 225-5701

Fourth District
Luis V. Gutierrez (D)
1208 Longworth House Office Building
Washington, DC 20515
Tel: (202) 225-8203

Fifth District
Dan Rostenkowski (D)
2111 Rayburn House Office Building
Washington, DC 20515
Tel: (202) 225-4061

Sixth District
Henry J. Hyde (R)
2110 Rayburn House Office Building
Washington, DC 20515
Tel: (202) 225-4561

Seventh District
Cardiss Collins (D)
2308 Rayburn House Office Building
Washington, DC 20515
Tel: (202) 225-5006

Eighth District
Philip M. Crane (R)
233 Cannon House Office Building
Washington, DC 20515
Tel: (202) 225-3711

Ninth District
Sidney R. Yates (D)
2109 Rayburn House Office Building
Washington, DC 20515
Tel: (202) 225-2111

Tenth District
John Edward Porter (R)
1026 Longworth House Office Building
Washington, DC 20515
Tel: (202) 225-4835

Eleventh District
George E. Sangmeister (D)
1032 Longworth House Office Building
Washington, DC 20515
Tel: (202) 225-3635

Twelfth District
Jerry F. Costello (D)
119 Cannon House Office Building
Washington, DC 20515
Tel: (202) 225-5661

Thirteenth District
Harris W. Fawell (R)
2342 Rayburn House Office Building
Washington, DC 20515
Tel: (202) 225-3515

Fourteenth District
J. Dennis Hastert (R)
2453 Rayburn House Office Building
Washington, DC 20515
Tel: (202) 225-2976

Fifteenth District
Thomas W. Ewing (R)
1317 Longworth House Office Building
Washington, DC 20515
Tel: (202) 225-2371

Sixteenth District
Donald Manzullo (R)
506 Cannon House Office Building
Washington, DC 20515
Tel: (202) 225-5676

Seventeenth District
Lane Evans (D)
2335 Rayburn House Office Building
Washington, DC 20515
Tel: (202) 225-5905

Eighteenth District
Robert H. Michel (R)
2112 Rayburn House Office Building
Washington, DC 20515
Tel: (202) 225-6201

Nineteenth District
Glenn Poshard (D)
107 Cannon House Office Building
Washington, DC 20515
Tel: (202) 225-5201

Twentieth District
Richard J. Durbin (D)
2463 Rayburn House Office Building
Washington, DC 20515
Tel: (202) 225-5271

INDIANA

First District
Peter J. Visclosky (D)
2464 Rayburn House Office Building
Washington, DC 20515
Tel: (202) 225-2461

Second District
Philip R. Sharp (D)
2217 Rayburn House Office Building
Washington, DC 20515
Tel: (202) 225-3021

Third District
Timothy J. Roemer (D)
415 Cannon House Office Building
Washington, DC 20515
Tel: (202) 225-3915

Fourth District
Jill L. Long (D)
1513 Longworth House Office Building
Washington, DC 20515
Tel: (202) 225-4436
Fifth District
Steve Buyer (R)
1419 Longworth House Office Building
Washington, DC 20515
Tel: (202) 225-5037

Sixth District
Dan Burton (R)
2411 Rayburn House Office Building
Washington, DC 20515
Tel: (202) 225-2276

Seventh District
John T. Myers (R)
2372 Rayburn House Office Building
Washington, DC 20515
Tel: (202) 225-4636

Eighth District
Frank McCloskey (D)
306 Cannon House Office Building
Washington, DC 20515
Tel: (202) 225-4636

Ninth District
Lee H. Hamilton (D)
2187 Rayburn House Office Building
Washington, DC 20515
Tel: (202) 225-5315

Tenth District
Andrew Jacobs, Jr. (D)
2313 Rayburn House Office Building
Washington, DC 20515
Tel: (202) 225-4011

IOWA

First District
James A. Leach (R)
2186 Rayburn House Office Building
Washington, DC 20515
Tel: (202) 225-6576

Second District
Jim Nussle (R)
308 Cannon House Office Building
Washington, DC 20515
Tel: (202) 225-2911

Third District
Jim Lightfoot (R)
2444 Rayburn House Office Building
Washington, DC 20515
Tel: (202) 225-3806
Fourth District
Neal Smith (D)
2373 Rayburn House Office Building
Washington, DC 20515
Tel: (202) 225-4426

Fifth District
Fred Grandy (R)
418 Cannon House Office Building
Washington, DC 20515
Tel: (202) 225-5476

KANSAS

First District
Pat Roberts (R)
1126 Longworth House Office Building
Washington, DC 20515
Tel: (202) 225-2715

Second District
Jim Slattery (D)
2243 Rayburn House Office Building
Washington, DC 20515
Tel: (202) 225-6601

Third District
Jan Meyers (R)
2338 Rayburn House Office Building
Washington, DC 20515
Tel: (202) 225-2865

Fourth District
Dan Glickman (D)
2371 Rayburn House Office Building
Washington, DC 20515
Tel: (202) 225-6216

KENTUCKY

First District
Tom Barlow (D)
1533 Longworth House Office Building
Washington, DC 20515
Tel: (202) 225-3115

Second District
William H. Natcher (D)
2333 Rayburn House Office Building

Washington, DC 20515
Tel: (202) 225-3501

Third District
Romano L. Mazzoli (D)
2246 Rayburn House Office Building
Washington, DC 20515
Tel: (202) 225-5401

Fourth District
Jim Bunning (R)
2437 Rayburn House Office Building
Washington, DC 20515
Tel: (202) 225-3465

Fifth District
Harold Rogers (R)
2468 Rayburn House Office Building
Washington, DC 20515
Tel: (202) 225-4601

Sixth District
Scotty Baesler (D)
508 Cannon House Office Building
Washington, DC 20515
Tel: (202) 225-4706

LOUISIANA

First District
Bob Livingston (R)
2368 Rayburn House Office Building
Washington, DC 20515
Tel: (202) 225-3015

Second District
William J. Jefferson (D)
428 Cannon House Office Building
Washington, DC 20515
Tel: (202) 225-6636

Third District
W.J. (Billy) Tauzin (D)
2330 Rayburn House Office Building
Washington, DC 20515
Tel: (202) 225-4031

Fourth District
Cleo Fields (D)
513 Cannon House Office Building
Washington, DC 20515
Tel: (202) 225-8490

Fifth District
Jim McCrery (R)
225 Cannon House Office Building
Washington, DC 20515
Tel: (202) 225-2777

Sixth District
Richard H. Baker (R)
434 Cannon House Office Building
Washington, DC 20515
Tel: (202) 225-3901

Seventh District
James A. Hayes (D)
2432 Rayburn House Office Building
Washington, DC 20515
Tel: (202) 225-2031

MAINE

First District
Thomas H. Andrews (D)
1530 Longworth House Office Building
Washington, DC 20515
Tel: (202) 225-6116

Second District
Olympia J. Snowe (R)
2268 Rayburn House Office Building
Washington, DC 20515
Tel: (202) 225-6306

MARYLAND

First District
Wayne T. Gilchrest (R)
412 Cannon House Office Building
Washington, DC 20515
Tel: (202) 225-5311

Second District
Helen Delich Bentley (R)
1610 Longworth House Office Building
Washington, DC 20515
Tel: (202) 225-3061

Third District
Benjamin L. Cardin (D)
227 Cannon House Office Building
Washington, DC 20515
Tel: (202) 225-4016

Fourth District

Albert R. Wynn (D)
423 Cannon House Office Building
Washington, DC 20515
Tel: (202) 225-8699

Fifth District
Steny H. Hoyer (D)
1705 Longworth House Office Building
Washington, DC 20515
Tel: (202) 225-4131

Sixth District
Roscoe G. Bartlett (R)
312 Cannon House Office Building
Washington, DC 20515
Tel: (202) 225-2721

Seventh District
Kweisi Mfume (D)
2419 Rayburn House Office Building
Washington, DC 20515
Tel: (202) 225-4741

Eight District
Constance A. Morella (R)
223 Cannon House Office Building
Washington, DC 20515
Tel: (202) 225-5341

MASSACHUSETTS

First District
John W. Oliver
1323 Longworth House Office Building
Washington, DC 20515
Tel: (202) 225-5335

Second District
Richard E. Neal (D)
131 Cannon House Office Building
Washington, DC 20515
Tel: (202) 225-5601

Third District
Peter I. Blute (R)
1029 Longworth House Office Building
Washington, DC 20515
Tel: (202) 225-6101

Fourth District
Barney Frank (D)
2404 Rayburn House Office Building
Washington, DC 20515
Tel: (202) 225-5931

Fifth District
Martin T. Meehan (D)
1223 Longworth House Office Building
Washington, DC 20515
Tel: (202) 225-3411

Sixth District
Peter G. Torkildsen (R)
120 Cannon House Office Building
Washington, DC 20515
Tel: (202) 225-8020

Seventh District
Edward J. Markey (D)
2133 Rayburn House Office Building
Washington, DC 20515
Tel: (202) 225-2836

Eighth District
Joseph P. Kennedy II (D)
1210 Longworth House Office Building
Washington, DC 20515
Tel: (202) 225-5111

Ninth District
John Joseph Moakley (D)
235 Cannon House Office Building
Washington, DC 20515
Tel: (202) 225-8273

Tenth District
Gerry E. Studds (D)
237 Cannon House Office Building
Washington, DC 20515
Tel: (202) 225-3111

MICHIGAN

First District
Bart T. Stupak (D)
317 Cannon House Office Building
Washington, DC 20515
Tel: (202) 225-4735

Second District
Peter Hoekstra (R)
1319 Longworth House Office Building
Washington, DC 20515
Tel: (202) 225-4401

Third District
Paul B. Henry (R)
1526 Longworth House Office Building
Washington, DC 20515

Tel: (202) 225-3831

Fourth District
Dave Camp (R)
137 Cannon House Office Building
Washington, DC 20515
Tel: (202) 225-3561

Fifth District
James A. Barcia (D)
1717 Longworth House Office Building
Washington, DC 20515
Tel: (202) 225-8171

Sixth District
Fred Upton (R)
2439 Rayburn House Office Building
Washington, DC 20515
Tel: (202) 225-3761

Seventh District
Nick Smith (R)
1708 Longworth House Office Building
Washington, DC 20515
Tel: (202) 225-6276

Eighth District
Bob Carr (D)
2347 Rayburn House Office Building
Washington, DC 20515
Tel: (202) 225-4872

Ninth District
Dale E. Kildee (D)
2239 Rayburn House Office Building
Washington, DC 20515
Tel: (202) 225-3611

Tenth District
David E. Bonior (D)
2207 Rayburn House Office Building
Washington, DC 20515
Tel: (202) 225-2106

Eleventh District
Joe Knollenberg (R)
1218 Longworth House Office Building
Washington, DC 20515
Tel: (202) 225-5802

Twelfth District
Sander M. Levin (D)
106 Cannon House Office Building
Washington, DC 20515
Tel: (202) 225-4961

Thirteenth District
William D. Ford (D)
2107 Rayburn House Office Building
Washington, DC 20515
Tel: (202) 225-6261

Fourteenth District
John Conyers, Jr. (D)
2426 Rayburn House Office Building
Washington, DC 20515
Tel: (202) 225-5126

Fifteenth District
Barbara-Rose Collins (D)
1108 Longworth House Office Building
Washington, DC 20515
Tel: (202) 225-2261

Sixteenth District
John D. Dingell
2328 Rayburn House Office Building
Washington, DC 20515
Tel: (202) 225-4071

MINNESOTA

First District
Timothy J. Penny (D)
436 Cannon House Office Building
Washington, DC 20515
Tel: (202) 225-2472

Second District
David Minge (D)
1508 Longworth House Office Building
Washington, DC 20515
Tel: (202) 225-2331

Third District
Jim Ramstad (R)
322 Cannon House Office Building
Washington, DC 20515
Tel: (202) 225-2871

Fourth District
Bruce F. Vento (D-Farmer-Labor)
2304 Rayburn House Office Building
Washington, DC 20515
Tel: (202) 225-6631

Fifth District

Martin Olav Sabo (D-Farmer-Labor)
2336 Rayburn House Office Building
Washington, DC 20515
Tel: (202) 225-4755

Sixth District
Rod Grams (R)
1713 Longworth House Office Building
Washington, DC 20515
Tel: (202) 225-2271

Seventh District
Collin C. Peterson (D)
1133 Longworth House Office Building
Washington, DC 20515
Tel: (202) 225-2165

Eighth District
James L. Oberstar (D)
2366 Rayburn House Office Building
Washington, DC 20515
Tel: (202) 225-6211

MISSISSIPPI

First District
Jamie L. Whitten (D)
2314 Rayburn House Office Building
Washington, DC 20515
Tel: (202) 225-4306

Second District
Bennie Thompson (D)
1408 Longworth House Office Building
Washington, DC 20515
Tel: (202) 225-5876

Third District
G.V. (Sonny) Montgomery (D)
2184 Rayburn House Office Building
Washington, DC 20515
Tel: (202) 225-5031

Fourth District
Mike Parker (D)
1410 Longworth House Office Building
Washington, DC 20515
Tel: (202) 225-5865

Fifth District
Gene Taylor (D)
215 Cannon House Office Building
Washington, DC 20515
Tel: (202) 225-5772

MISSOURI

First District
William (Bill) Clay (D)
2306 Rayburn House Office Building
Washington, DC 20515
Tel: (202) 225-2406

Second District
James M. Talent (R)
1022 Longworth House Office Building
Washington, DC 20515
Tel: (202) 225-2561

Third District
Richard A. Gephardt (D)
1432 Longworth House Office Building
Washington, DC 20515
Tel: (202) 225-2671

Fourth District
Ike Skelton (D)
2227 Rayburn House Office Building
Washington, DC 20515
Tel: (202) 225-2876

Fifth District
Alan Wheat (D)
2334 Rayburn House Office Building
Washington, DC 20515
Tel: (202) 225-4535

Sixth District
Pat Danner (D)
1217 Longworth House Office Building
Washington, DC 20515
Tel: (202) 225-7041

Seventh District
Mel Hancock (R)
129 Cannon House Office Building
Washington, DC 20515
Tel: (202) 225-6536

Eighth District
Bill Emerson (R)
2454 Rayburn House Office Building
Washington, DC 20515
Tel: (202) 225-4404

Ninth District
Harold L. Volkmer (D)
2409 Rayburn House Office Building

Washington, DC 20515
Tel: (202) 225-2956

MONTANA

At Large
Pat Williams (D)
2457 Rayburn House Office Building
Washington, DC 20515
Tel: (202) 225-3211

NEBRASKA

First District
Doug Bereuter (R)
2348 Rayburn House Office Building
Washington, DC 20515
Tel: (202) 225-4806

Second District
Peter Hoagland (D)
1113 Longworth House Office Building
Washington, DC 20515
Tel: (202) 225-4155

Third District
Bill Barrett (R)
1213 Longworth House Office Building
Washington, DC 20515
Tel: (202) 225-6435

NEVADA

First District
James H. Bilbray (D)
2431 Rayburn House Office Building
Washington, DC 20515
Tel: (202) 225-5965

Second District
Barbara F. Vucanovich (R)
2202 Rayburn House Office Building
Washington, DC 20515
Tel: (202) 225-6155

NEW HAMPSHIRE

First District
Bill Zeliff, Jr. (R)
224 Cannon House Office Building
Washington, DC 20515
Tel: (202) 225-5456

Second District
Dick Swett (D)
230 Cannon House Office Building
Washington, DC 20515
Tel: (202) 225-5206

NEW JERSEY

First District
Robert E. Andrews (D)
1005 Longworth House Office Building
Washington, DC 20515
Tel: (202) 225-6501

Second District
William J. Hughes (D)
241 Cannon House Office Building
Washington, DC 20515
Tel: (202) 225-6572

Third District
Jim Saxton (R)
438 Cannon House Office Building
Washington, DC 20515
Tel: (202) 225-4765

Fourth District
Christopher H. Smith (R)
2353 Rayburn House Office Building
Washington, DC 20515
Tel: (202) 225-3765

Fifth District
Marge Roukema (R)
2244 Rayburn House Office Building
Washington, DC 20515
Tel: (202) 225-4465

Sixth District
Frank Pallone, Jr. (D)
420 Cannon House Office Building
Washington, DC 20515
Tel: (202) 225-4671

Seventh District
Bob Franks (R)
429 Cannon House Office Building
Washington, DC 20515
Tel: (202) 225-5361

Eighth District
Herbert C. Klein (D)
1728 Longworth House Office Building
Washington, DC 20515
Tel: (202) 225-5751

Ninth District

Robert G. Torricelli (D)
2159 Rayburn House Office Building
Washington, DC 20515
Tel: (202) 225-5061

Tenth District
Donald M. Payne (D)
417 Cannon House Office Building
Washington, DC 20515
Tel: (202) 225-3436

Eleventh District
Dean A. Gallo (R)
2447 Rayburn House Office Building
Washington, DC 20515
Tel: (202) 225-5034

Twelfth District
Dick Zimmer (R)
228 Cannon House Office Building
Washington, DC 20515
Tel: (202) 225-5801

Thirteenth District
Robert Menendez (D)
1531 Longworth House Office Building
Washington, DC 20515
Tel: (202) 225-7919

NEW MEXICO

First District
Steven Schiff (R)
1009 Longworth House Office Building
Washington, DC 20515
Tel: (202) 225-6316

Second District
Joe Skeen (R)
2367 Rayburn House Office Building
Washington, DC 20515
Tel: (202) 225-2365

Third District
Bill Richardson (D)
2349 Rayburn House Office Building
Washington, DC 20515
Tel: (202) 225-6190

NEW YORK

First District
George J. Hochbrueckner (D)
229 Cannon House Office Building
Washington, DC 20515
Tel: (202) 225-3826

Second District
Rick A. Lazio (R)
314 Cannon House Office Building
Washington, DC 20515
Tel: (202) 225-3335

Third District
Peter T. King (R)
118 Cannon House Office Building
Washington, DC 20515
Tel: (202) 225-7896

Fourth District
David A. Levy (R)
116 Cannon House Office Building
Washington, DC 20515
Tel: (202) 225-5516

Fifth District
Gary L. Ackerman (D)
2445 Rayburn House Office Building
Washington, DC 20515
Tel: (202) 225-2601

Sixth District
Floyd H. Flake (D)
1035 Longworth House Office Building
Washington, DC 20515
Tel: (202) 225-3461

Seventh District
Thomas J. Manton (D)
203 Cannon House Office Building
Washington, DC 20515
Tel: (202) 225-3965

Eighth District
Jerrold Nadler (D)
424 Cannon House Office Building
Washington, DC 20515
Tel: (202) 225-5635

Ninth District
Charles E. Schumer (D)
2412 Rayburn House Office Building
Washington, DC 20515
Tel: (202) 225-6616

Tenth District
Edolphus Towns (D)

2232 Rayburn House Office Building
Washington, DC 20515
Tel: (202) 225-5936

Eleventh District
Major R. Owens (D)
2305 Rayburn House Office Building
Washington, DC 20515
Tel: (202) 225-6231

Twelfth District
Nydia M. Velazquez (D)
132 Cannon House Office Building
Washington, DC 20515
Tel: (202) 225-2361

Thirteenth District
Susan Molinari (R)
123 Cannon House Office Building
Washington, DC 20515
Tel: (202) 225-3371

Fourteenth District
Carolyn B. Maloney (D)
1504 Longworth House Office Building
Washington, DC 20515
Tel: (202) 225-7944

Fifteenth District
Charles B. Rangel (D)
2252 Rayburn House Office Building
Washington, DC 20515
Tel: (202) 225-4365

Sixteenth District
Jose E. Serrano (D)
336 Cannon House Office Building
Washington, DC 20515
Tel: (202) 225-4361

Seventeenth District
Eliot L. Engel (D)
1433 Longworth House Office Building
Washington, DC 20515
Tel: (202) 225-2464

Eighteenth District
Nita M. Lowey (D)
1424 Longworth House Office Building
Washington, DC 20515
Tel: (202) 225-6506

Nineteenth District
Hamilton Fish, Jr. (R)
2354 Rayburn House Office Building
Washington, DC 20515
Tel: (202) 225-5441

Twentieth District
Benjamin A. Gilman (R)
2185 Rayburn House Office Building
Washington, DC 20515
Tel: (202) 225-3776

Twenty-First District
Michael R. McNulty (D)
217 Cannon House Office Building
Washington, DC 20515
Tel: (202) 225-5076

Twenty-Second District
Gerald B.H. Solomon (R)
2265 Rayburn House Office Building
Washington, DC 20515
Tel: (202) 225-5614

Twenty-Third District
Sherwood L. Boehlert (R)
1127 Longworth House Office Building
Washington, DC 20515
Tel: (202) 225-3665

Twenty-Fourth District
John M. McHugh (R)
416 Cannon House Office Building
Washington, DC 20515
Tel: (202) 225-4611

Twenty-Fifth District
James T. Walsh (R)
1330 Longworth House Office Building
Washington, DC 20515
Tel: (202) 225-3701

Twenty-Sixth District
Maurice D. Hinchey (D)
1313 Longworth House Office Building
Washington, DC 20515
Tel: (202) 225-6335

Twenty-Seventh District
Bill Paxon (R)
1314 Longworth House Office Building
Washington, DC 20515
Tel: (202) 225-5265

Twenty-Eighth District

Louise McIntosh Slaughter (D)
2421 Rayburn House Office Building
Washington, DC 20515
Tel: (202) 225-3615

Twenty-Ninth District
John J. LaFalce (D)
2310 Rayburn House Office Building
Washington, DC 20515
Tel: (202) 225-3231

Thirtieth District
Jack Quinn (R)
331 Cannon House Office Building
Washington, DC 20515
Tel: (202) 225-3306

Thirty-First District
Amo Houghton (R)
1110 Longworth House Office Building
Washington, DC 20515
Tel: (202) 225-3161

NORTH CAROLINA

First District
Eva Clayton (D)
222 Cannon House Office Building
Washington, DC 20515
Tel: (202) 225-3101

Second District
Tim Valentine (D)
2229 Rayburn House Office Building
Washington, DC 20515
Tel: (202) 225-4531

Third District
H. Martin Lancaster (D)
2436 Rayburn House Office Building
Washington, DC 20515
Tel: (202) 225-3415

Fourth District
David E. Price (D)
2458 Rayburn House Office Building
Washington, DC 20515
Tel: (202) 225-1784

Fifth District
Stephen L. Neal (D)
2469 Rayburn House Office Building
Washington, DC 20515
Tel: (202) 225-2071

Sixth District
Howard Coble (R)
403 Cannon House Office Building
Washington, DC 20515
Tel: (202) 225-3065

Seventh District
Charlie Rose (D)
2230 Rayburn House Office Building
Washington, DC 20515
Tel: (202) 225-2731

Eighth District
W.G. (Bill) Hefner (D)
2470 Rayburn House Office Building
Washington, DC 20515
Tel: (202) 225-3715

Ninth District
J. Alex McMillan (R)
401 Cannon House Office Building
Washington, DC 20515
Tel: (202) 225-1976

Tenth District
Cass Ballenger (R)
2238 Rayburn House Office Building
Washington, DC 20515
Tel: (202) 225-2576

Eleventh District
Charles H. Taylor (R)
516 Cannon House Office Building
Washington, DC 20515
Tel: (202) 225-6401

Twelfth District
Melvin Watt (D)
1232 Longworth House Office Building
Washington, DC 20515
Tel: (202) 225-1510

NORTH DAKOTA

At Large
Earl Ralph Pomeroy (Democrat-NPL)
318 Cannon House Office Building
Washington, DC 20515
Tel: (202) 225-2611

OHIO

First District
David Mann (D)

503 Cannon House Office Building
Washington, DC 20515
Tel: (202) 225-2216

Second District
Rob Portman (R)
238 Cannon House Office Building
Washington, DC 20515
Tel: (202) 225-3164

Third District
Tony P. Hall (D)
2264 Rayburn House Office Building
Washington, DC 20515
Tel: (202) 225-6465

Fourth District
Michael G. Oxley (R)
2233 Rayburn House Office Building
Washington, DC 20515
Tel: (202) 225-2676

Fifth District
Paul E. Gillmor (R)
1203 Longworth House Office Building
Washington, DC 20515
Tel: (202) 225-6405

Sixth District
Ted Strickland (D)
1429 Longworth House Office Building
Washington, DC 20515
Tel: (202) 225-5705

Seventh District
David L. Hobson (R)
1507 Longworth House Office Building
Washington, DC 20515
Tel: (202) 225-4324

Eighth District
John A. Boehner (R)
1020 Longworth House Office Building
Washington, DC 20515
Tel: (202) 225-6205

Ninth District
Marcy Kaptur (D)
2104 Rayburn House Office Building
Washington, DC 20515
Tel: (202) 225-4146

Tenth District
Martin R. Hoke (R)
212 Cannon House Office Building
Washington, DC 20515
Tel: (202) 225-5871

Eleventh District
Louis Stokes (D)
2365 Rayburn House Office Building
Washington, DC 20515
Tel: (202) 225-7032

Twelfth District
John R. Kasich (R)
1131 Longworth House Office Building
Washington, DC 20515
Tel: (202) 225-5355

Thirteenth District
Sherrod Brown (D)
1407 Longworth House Office Building
Washington, DC 20515
Tel: (202) 225-3401

Fourteenth District
Thomas C. Sawyer (D)
1414 Longworth House Office Building
Washington, DC 20515
Tel: (202) 225-5231

Fifteenth District
Deborah Pryce (R)
128 Cannon House Office Building
Washington, DC 20515
Tel: (202) 225-2015

Sixteenth District
Ralph Regula (R)
2309 Rayburn House Office Building
Washington, DC 20515
Tel: (202) 225-3876

Seventeenth District
James A. Traficant, Jr. (D)
2446 Rayburn House Office Building
Washington, DC 20515
Tel: (202) 225-5261

Eighteenth District
Douglas Applegate (D)
2183 Rayburn House Office Building
Washington, DC 20515
Tel: (202) 225-6265

Nineteenth District
Eric D. Fingerhut (D)
431 Cannon House Office Building
Washington, DC 20515
Tel: (202) 225-5731

OKLAHOMA

First District
James M. Inhofe (R)
442 Cannon House Office Building
Washington, DC 20515
Tel: (202) 225-2211

Second District
Mike Synar (D)
2329 Rayburn House Office Building
Washington, DC 20515
Tel: (202) 225-2701

Third District
Bill Brewster (D)
1727 Longworth House Office Building
Washington, DC 20515
Tel: (202) 225-4565

Fourth District
Dave McCurdy (D)
2344 Rayburn House Office Building
Washington, DC 20515
Tel: (202) 225-6165

Fifth District
Ernest J. Istook, Jr. (R)
1116 Longworth House Office Building
Washington, DC 20515
Tel: (202) 225-2132

Sixth District
Glenn English (D)
2206 Rayburn House Office Building
Washington, DC 20515
Tel: (202) 225-5565

OREGON

First District
Elizabeth Furse (D)
316 Cannon House Office Building
Washington, DC 20515
Tel: (202) 225-0855

Second District
Robert F. (Bob) Smith (R)
108 Cannon House Office Building
Washington, DC 20515
Tel: (202) 225-6730

Third District
Ron Wyden (D)
1111 Longworth House Office Building
Washington, DC 20515
Tel: (202) 225-4811

Fourth District
Peter A. DeFazio (D)
1233 Longworth House Office Building
Washington, DC 20515
Tel: (202) 225-6416

Fifth District
Mike Kopetski (D)
218 Cannon House Office Building
Washington, DC 20515
Tel: (202) 225-5711

PENNSYLVANIA

First District
Thomas M. Foglietta (D)
341 Cannon House Office Building
Washington, DC 20515
Tel: (202) 225-4731

Second District
Lucien E. Blackwell (D)
410 Cannon House Office Building
Washington, DC 20515
Tel: (202) 225-4001

Third District
Robert A. Borski (D)
2161 Rayburn House Office Building
Washington, DC 20515
Tel: (202) 225-8251

Fourth District
Ron Klink (D)
1130 Longworth House Office Building
Washington, DC 20515
Tel: (202) 225-2565

Fifth District
William F. Clinger, Jr. (R)
2160 Rayburn House Office Building
Washington, DC 20515
Tel: (202) 225-5121

Sixth District
Tim Holden (D)
1421 Longworth House Office Building
Washington, DC 20515

Tel: (202) 225-5546

Seventh District
Curt Weldon (R)
2452 Rayburn House Office Building
Washington, DC 20515
Tel: (202) 225-2011

Eighth District
James C. Greenwood (R)
515 Cannon House Office Building
Washington, DC 20515
Tel: (202) 225-4276

Ninth District
Bud Shuster (R)
2188 Rayburn House Office Building
Washington, DC 20515
Tel: (202) 225-2431

Tenth District
Joseph M. McDade (R)
2370 Rayburn House Office Building
Washington, DC 20515
Tel: (202) 225-3731

Eleventh District
Paul E. Kanjorski (D)
2429 Rayburn House Office Building
Washington, DC 20515
Tel: (202) 225-6511

Twelfth District
John P. Murtha (D)
2423 Rayburn House Office Building
Washington, DC 20515
Tel: (202) 225-2065

Thirteenth District
Marjorie Margolies-Mezvinsky (D)
1516 Longworth House Office Building
Washington, DC 20515
Tel: (202) 225-6111

Fourteenth District
William J. Coyne (D)
2455 Rayburn House Office Building
Washington, DC 20515
Tel: (202) 225-2301

Fifteenth District
Paul McHale (D)
511 Cannon House Office Building
Washington, DC 20515
Tel: (202) 225-6411

Sixteenth District
Robert S. Walker (R)
2369 Rayburn House Office Building
Washington, DC 20515
Tel: (202) 225-2411

Seventeenth District
George Gekas (R)
2410 Rayburn House Office Building
Washington, DC 20515
Tel: (202) 225-4315

Eighteenth District
Rick Santorum (R)
1222 Longworth House Office Building
Washington, DC 20515
Tel: (202) 225-2135

Nineteenth District
William F. Goodling (R)
2263 Rayburn House Office Building
Washington, DC 20515
Tel: (202) 225-5836

Twentieth District
Austin J. Murphy (D)
2210 Rayburn House Office Building
Washington, DC 20515
Tel: (202) 225-4665

Twenty-First District
Thomas J. Ridge (R)
1714 Longworth House Office Building
Washington, DC 20515
Tel: (202) 225-5406

RHODE ISLAND

First District
Ronald K. Machtley (R)
326 Cannon House Office Building
Washington, DC 20515
Tel: (202) 225-4911

Second District
Jack Reed (D)
1510 Longworth House Office Building
Washington, DC 20515
Tel: (202) 225-2735

SOUTH CAROLINA

First District
Arthur Ravenel, Jr. (R)
231 Cannon House Office Building
Washington, DC 20515
Tel: (202) 225-3176

Second District
Floyd Spence (R)
2405 Rayburn House Office Building
Washington, DC 20515
Tel: (202) 225-2452

Third District
Butler C. Derrick, Jr. (D)
221 Cannon House Office Building
Washington, DC 20515
Tel: (202) 225-5301

Fourth District
Bob Inglis (R)
1237 Longworth House Office Building
Washington, DC 20515
Tel: (202) 225-6030

Fifth District
John M. Spratt, Jr. (D)
1536 Longworth House Office Building
Washington, DC 20515
Tel: (202) 225-5501

Sixth District
James E. Clyburn (D)
319 Cannon House Office Building
Washington, DC 20515
Tel: (202) 225-3315

SOUTH DAKOTA

At Large
Tim Johnson (D)
2438 Rayburn House Office Building
Washington, DC 20515
Tel: (202) 225-2801

TENNESSEE

First District
James H. (Jimmy) Quillen (R)
102 Cannon House Office Building
Washington, DC 20515
Tel: (202) 225-6356

Second District
John J. Duncan, Jr. (R)
115 Cannon House Office Building
Washington, DC 20515
Tel: (202) 225-5435

Third District
Marilyn Lloyd (D)
2406 Rayburn House Office Building
Washington, DC 20515
Tel: (202) 225-3271

Fourth District
Jim Cooper (D)
125 Cannon House Office Building
Washington, DC 20515
Tel: (202) 225-6831

Fifth District
Bob Clement (D)
1230 Longworth House Office Building
Washington, DC 20515
Tel: (202) 225-4311

Sixth District
Bart Gordon (D)
103 Cannon House Office Building
Washington, DC 20515
Tel: (202) 225-4231

Seventh District
Don Sundquist (R)
339 Cannon House Office Building
Washington, DC 20515
Tel: (202) 225-2811

Eighth District
John S. Tanner (D)
1427 Longworth House Office Building
Washington, DC 20515
Tel: (202) 225-4714

Ninth District
Harold E. Ford (D)
2211 Rayburn House Office Building
Washington, DC 20515
Tel: (202) 225-3265

TEXAS

First District

Jim Chapman (D)
2417 Rayburn House Office Building
Washington, DC 20515
Tel: (202) 225-3035

Second District
Charles Wilson (D)
2256 Rayburn House Office Building
Washington, DC 20515
Tel: (202) 225-2401

Third District
Sam Johnson (R)
1030 Longworth House Office Building
Washington, DC 20515
Tel: (202) 225-4201

Fourth District
Ralph M. Hall (D)
2236 Rayburn House Office Building
Washington, DC 20515
Tel: (202) 225-6673

Fifth District
John Bryant (D)
205 Cannon House Office Building
Washington, DC 20515
Tel: (202) 225-2231

Sixth District
Joe Barton (R)
1514 Longworth House Office Building
Washington, DC 20515
Tel: (202) 225-2002

Seventh District
Bill Archer (R)
1236 Longworth House Office Building
Washington, DC 20515
Tel: (202) 225-2571

Eighth District
Jack M. Fields, Jr. (R)
2228 Rayburn House Office Building
Washington, DC 20515
Tel: (202) 225-4901

Ninth District
Jack Brooks (D)
2449 Rayburn House Office Building
Washington, DC 20515
Tel: (202) 225-6565

Tenth District
J.J. Pickle (D)
242 Cannon House Office Building
Washington, DC 20515
Tel: (202) 225-4865

Eleventh District
Chet Edwards (D)
328 Cannon House Office Building
Washington, DC 20515
Tel: (202) 225-6105

Twelfth District
Pete Geren (D)
1730 Longworth House Office Building
Washington, DC 20515
Tel: (202) 225-5071

Thirteenth District
Bill Sarpaulius (D)
126 Cannon House Office Building
Washington, DC 20515
Tel: (202) 225-3706

Fourteenth District
Greg Laughlin (D)
236 Cannon House Office Building
Washington, DC 20515
Tel: (202) 225-2831

Fifteenth District
E (Kika) DE LA Garza (D)
1401 Longworth House Office Building
Washington, DC 20515
Tel: (202) 225-2531

Sixteenth District
Ronald D. Coleman (D)
440 Cannon House Office Building
Washington, DC 20515
Tel: (202) 225-4831

Seventeenth District
Charles W. Stenholm (D)
1211 Longworth House Office Building
Washington, DC 20515
Tel: (202) 225-6605

Eighteenth District

Craig A. Washington (D)
1711 Longworth House Office Building
Washington, DC 20515
Tel: (202) 225-3816

Nineteenth District
Larry Combest (R)
1511 Longworth House Office Building
Washington, DC 20515
Tel: (202) 225-4005

Twentieth District
Henry B. Gonzalez (D)
2413 Rayburn House Office Building
Washington, DC 20515
Tel: (202) 225-3236

Twenty-First District
Lamar Smith (R)
2443 Rayburn House Office Building
Washington, DC 20515
Tel: (202) 225-4236

Twenty-Second District
Tom DeLay (R)
407 Cannon House Office Building
Washington, DC 20515
Tel: (202) 225-5951

Twenty-Third District
Henry Bonilla (R)
1529 Longworth House Office Building
Washington, DC 20515
Tel: (202) 225-4511

Twenty-Fourth District
Martin Frost (D)
2459 Rayburn House Office Building
Washington, DC 20515
Tel: (202) 225-3605

Twenty-Fifth District
Michael A. Andrews (D)
303 Cannon House Office Building
Washington, DC 20515
Tel: (202) 225-7508

Twenty-Sixth District
Dick Armey (R)
301 Cannon House Office Building
Washington, DC 20515
Tel: (202) 225-7772

Twenty-Seventh District
Solomon P. Ortiz (D)
2136 Rayburn House Office Building
Washington, DC 20515
Tel: (202) 225-7742

Twenty-Eighth District
Frank M. Tejeda (D)
323 Cannon House Office Building
Washington, DC 20515
Tel: (202) 225-1640

Twenty-Ninth District
Gene Green (D)
1004 Longworth House Office Building
Washington, DC 20515
Tel: (202) 225-1688

Thirtieth District
Eddie Bernice Johnson (D)
1721 Longworth House Office Building
Washington, DC 20515
Tel: (202) 225-8885

UTAH

First District
James V. Hansen (R)
2466 Rayburn House Office Building
Washington, DC 20515
Tel: (202) 225-0453

Second District
Karen Shepherd (D)
414 Cannon House Office Building
Washington, DC 20515
Tel: (202) 225-3011

Third District
Bill Orton (D)
1122 Longworth House Office Building
Washington, DC 20515
Tel: (202) 225-7751

VERMONT

At Large
Bernard Sanders (I)
213 Cannon House Office Building
Washington, DC 20515
Tel: (202) 225-4115

VIRGINIA

First District
Herbert H. Bateman (R)

2350 Rayburn House Office Building
Washington, DC 20515
Tel: (202) 225-4024

Second District
Owen B. Pickett (D)
2430 Rayburn House Office Building
Washington, DC 20515
Tel: (202) 225-4215

Third District
Robert C. (Bobby) Scott (D)
501 Cannon House Office Building
Washington, DC 20515
Tel: (202) 225-8351

Fourth District
Norman Sisisky (D)
2352 Rayburn House Office Building
Washington, DC 20515
Tel: (202) 225-6365

Fifth District
Lewis F. Payne, Jr. (D)
1119 Longworth House Office Building
Washington, DC 20515
Tel: (202) 225-4711

Sixth District
Robert W. (Bob) Goodlatte (R)
214 Cannon House Office Building
Washington, DC 20515
Tel: (202) 225-5431

Seventh District
Thomas J. Bliley, Jr. (R)
2241 Rayburn House Office Building
Washington, DC 20515
Tel: (202) 225-2815

Eighth District
James P. Moran (D)
430 Cannon House Office Building
Washington, DC 20515
Tel: (202) 225-4376

Ninth District
Rick Boucher (D)
2245 Rayburn House Office Building
Washington, DC 20515
Tel: (202) 225-3861

Tenth District
Frank R. Wolf (R)
104 Cannon House Office Building
Washington, DC 20515
Tel: (202) 225-5136

Eleventh District
Leslie L. Byrne (D)
1609 Longworth House Office Building
Washington, DC 20515
Tel: (202) 225-1492

WASHINGTON

First District
Maria Cantwell (D)
1520 Longworth House Office Building
Washington, DC 20515
Tel: (202) 225-6311

Second District
Al Swift (D)
1502 Longworth House Office Building
Washington, DC 20515
Tel: (202) 225-2605

Third District
Jolene Unsoeld (D)
1527 Longworth House Office Building
Washington, DC 20515
Tel: (202) 225-3536

Fourth District
Jay Inslee (D)
1431 Longworth House Office Building
Washington, DC 20515
Tel: (202) 225-5816

Fifth District
Thomas S. Foley (D)
1201 Longworth House Office Building
Washington, DC 20515
Tel: (202) 225-2006

Sixth District
Norman D. Dicks (D)
2467 Rayburn House Office Building
Washington, DC 20515
Tel: (202) 225-5916

Seventh District
Jim McDermott (D)
1707 Longworth House Office Building
Washington, DC 20515
Tel: (202) 225-3106

Eighth District

Jennifer Dunn (R)
1641 Longworth House Office Building
Washington, DC 20515
Tel: (202) 225-7761

Ninth District
Mike Kreidler (D)
1535 Longworth House Office Building
Washington, DC 20515
Tel: (202) 225-8901

WEST VIRGINIA

First District
Alan B. Mollohan (D)
2242 Rayburn House Office Building
Washington, DC 20515
Tel: (202) 225-4172

Second District
Robert E. Wise, Jr. (D)
2434 Rayburn House Office Building
Washington, DC 20515
Tel: (202) 225-2711

Third District
Nick Rahall II (D)
2269 Rayburn House Office Building
Washington, DC 20515
Tel: (202) 225-3452

WISCONSIN

First District
Peter Barca (D)
1719 Longworth House Office Building
Washington, DC 20515
Tel: (202) 225-3031

Second District
Scott Klug (R)
1224 Longworth House Office Building
Washington, DC 20515
Tel: (202) 225-2906

Third District
Steve Gunderson (R)
2235 Rayburn House Office Building
Washington, DC 20515
Tel: (202) 225-5506

Fourth District
Gerald D. Kleczka (D)
2301 Rayburn House Office Building
Washington, DC 20515
Tel: (202) 225-4572

Fifth District
Thomas M. Barrett (D)
313 Cannon House Office Building
Washington, DC 20515
Tel: (202) 225-3571

Sixth District
Thomas E. Petri (R)
2262 Rayburn House Office Building
Washington, DC 20515
Tel: (202) 225-2476

Seventh District
David R. Obey (D)
2462 Rayburn House Office Building
Washington, DC 20515
Tel: (202) 225-3365

Eighth District
Toby Roth (R)
2234 Rayburn House Office Building
Washington, DC 20515
Tel: (202) 225-5665

Ninth District
F. James Sensenbrenner, Jr. (R)
2332 Rayburn House Office Building
Washington, DC 20515
Tel: (202) 225-5101

WYOMING

At Large
Craig Thomas (R)
1019 Longworth House Office Building
Washington, DC 20515
Tel: (202) 225-2311

AMERICAN SAMOA

Delegate
Eni F.H. Faleomavaega (D)
109 Cannon House Office Building
Washington, DC 20515
Tel: (202) 225-8577

DISTRICT OF COLUMBIA

Delegate
Eleanor Holmes Norton (D)
1415 Longworth House Office Building
Washington, DC 20515
Tel: (202) 225-8050

GUAM

Delegate
Robert A. Underwood (D)
507 Cannon House Office Building

Washington, DC 20515
Tel: (202) 225-1188

PUERTO RICO

Resident Commissioner
Carlos Romero-Barcelo (D)
1517 Longworth House Office Building
Washington, DC 20515
Tel: (202) 225-2615

VIRGIN ISLANDS

Delegate
Ron de Lugo (D)
2427 Rayburn House Office Building
Washington, DC 20515
Tel: (202) 225-1790

CONTENTS

PART III

APPENDICES